AWAKE
IN THE
SPIRIT

M. BASIL PENNINGTON, O.C.S.O.

AWAKE
IN THE
SPIRIT

A Personal Handbook on Prayer

CROSSROAD • NEW YORK

1997

The Crossroad Publishing Company
370 Lexington Avenue, New York, NY 10017

Printed in the United States of America

Library of Congress Cataloging-in-Publication Data

Pennington, M. Basil.
    Awake in the spirit : a personal handbook on prayer / M. Basil
Pennington.
        p. cm.
    Includes bibliographical references.
    ISBN 0-8245-1167-0 (hard); 0-8245-1516-1 (pbk.)
    1. Prayer. 2. Spiritual life—Catholic authors. I. Title.
BV215.P45 1992
248.3'2—dc20   92-9443
                                                            CIP

To the
Monks
of
OUR LADY OF JOY
Martyrs and Confessors
who have kept the Cistercian life alive in China
through forty years of persecution and exile.

CONTENTS

PREFACE

Everyone is seeking him — or her or it. The twelve-step program refers to them as the Higher Power. Whatever the denomination, there is deep within every one of us a great longing, a deep desire, a thirst, we might say, for something, for someone who can fill us.

Blessed are those who have been gifted with parents or guardians, masters or pastors who have helped them to interpret this deep longing and need, and better, have pointed the way and guided and aided. Unfortunately most have not been so blessed. All too often there has been no modeling save the modeling of a life spent in trying to escape the angst of an unfilled longing through the blur of alcohol or the high of drugs, the ephemeral excitement and warmth of sex or the distracting boredom of television.

Sad to say, even when there has been some good guidance, where one has been born into a household of faith, a community of believers, all too often the way to fulfillment has not been truly or effectively offered. Rather religion has been set forth as doings and duties that seek more to abate rather than fulfill these deep longings. If the longing or need still manages to assert itself in the midst of our doings, they promise fulfill-ment "later on." Young questing minds and hearts as well as those of later years who have been awakened one way or another—perhaps by the mid-life crisis— are not so easily deceived by this subterfuge. They see no meaning in the doings and duties if these do not in some way begin to respond to the deep longings within.

The deep need we feel when we are most open and vulnerable, most present to ourselves, is written in our very nature. We are made to know the real meaning of our life and its journey, to be in touch with our source, to see our end and to be fulfilled by it. As long as hope is within us, we seek to find the answers or to find someone who might have the answers, not in theory or concepts but experientially, in living reality.

In recent years we have seen many young and not so young make the pilgrimage east, seeking in hope one who has some answers, who knows the way. This is not a new phenomenon. Rather it is one that has been present all throughout history. Eyes have turned to the East and feet have followed in hope.

Two young fishermen, laboring with their families on the Sea of Galilee, had been hearing rumors. There was said to be a prophet out there in the desert, east of the Jordan. These were Jewish lads, men of faith. And their faith was filled with prophets. But not their times. They wanted something more, these lively young men; they wanted to be fulfilled. Perhaps..., perhaps that man out there was the One. Soon they left their fathers and their nets and headed east. They found the strange man from the desert, a wiry, bronzed figure, clothed in the hide of a camel, satisfying his hunger with locusts and wild honey, and preaching fire and conversion and waters of baptism. The young men asked him, straightforward: Are you the One? Or are we to look for another? And the Baptizer answered them equally straightforward: I am not the One. But wait; he is coming.

And they waited.

Then one day, as the Baptizer was excoriating the crowd who had come out to him, he suddenly stopped. His eyes glistened. His arm raised in salute. His finger pointed. "There, there is the Lamb of God."

The two young men from the shores of Galilee, Andrew and John, did not hesitate. Immediately they made their way through the crowd and hastened after the disappearing figure. As they came up behind him, he turned and spoke to them. His question is the first recorded words of our Savior to his disciples: "What do you want? What are you seeking?"

John was a true seeker. He wanted all the Teacher had to offer. And nothing less. "Where do you dwell?" John was ready to move in. The Lord's answer, as always, was inviting: "Come and see."

I have little doubt that John and Andrew fully expected the Lord to lead them to some humble abode or rich benefactor's home, where they could sit quietly at his feet and learn the way. Instead they learned something else. They learned that, while foxes have their dens and birds of the air their nests, the Son of

Man had not whereon to lay his head. Nonetheless,
they followed, these seekers. They followed the Master
day and night, week in and week out, month in and
month out, year in and year out.

Finally, on the night before he was to die, the night
on which he most fully opened his heart to these
chosen ones — and to us — Jesus answered John's
question. Once again that special Greek word that
speaks of dwelling, of being at home with those you
love, appears. And the Master tells John: "The Father
and I will dwell in you."

Where does God dwell? God is everywhere — always
and at all times. But where does God dwell in intimacy with those whom God loves? Where does God
make a home in this world? God dwells in you and
me. What so many seek outside, in so many doings
and havings, is already with us within. As Jesus said
on another occasion: The Reign of God is within.

What we seek — the Higher Power, the Source of our
being, the Source of all life and love — is within. God
dwells within us, the God who made us and who is
the fulfillment of all our longings. As one great seeker,
who followed many a wrong path before he came to
the true way, has well put it: "Our hearts are made for
you, O Lord, and they will not rest until they rest in
you."

The God we seek is within. The Spirit, the Paraclete
who will teach us all things, abides within us. What we
seek or whom we seek is within. And this book is about
effective ways that men and women of the Christian
tradition have through the centuries used to awaken

to the God within, so that their deepest longings, their most ardent desires might be fulfilled.

We do not intend to present these ways only as historical realities. We will present them as ways that we can easily make part of our own journey today. The practices have helped saints, great and less great, known and unknown, of times long past and of our own times, awaken to the Spirit within and find the fulfillment of their heart's desire, find the true meaning of their existence and the fulfillment of that. I am sure that these ways can help us today, to whatever extent we want to let them. They are ours, a gift of the ages, to be used as we like. May they bring us much joy and peace and fulfillment.

M. Basil Pennington, O.C.S.O.
Our Lady of Joy Priory
Lantao Island, Hong Kong
Feast of All Saints

AWAKE
IN THE
SPIRIT

CHAPTER ONE

LISTENING

I have listened to many hearts over the decades. I have dared at times to listen deeply to my own heart. What I have heard there within my own heart I do not think differs from what I hear in other hearts — albeit sometimes underneath many, many thoughts, ideas, concepts, rationalizations, and images. I hear hearts longing for a love big enough for them. A love that will be permanent and steadfast. A love that will not waver. A love that will be all-embracing, even while it penetrates to the very depths of our being and sees open before it all our misery and meanness. A love that, we must admit, seems to us to be an almost unbelievable love. But we want a love that does not need to be believed, we want one that will be known and known to be true. We long for such a love, and yet it must be a two-way love. We want such an incredible lover and we want that incredible lover to want our love in return.

18

No wonder we hide such longings deep within, beneath many layers of considerations and doings. It is
too much of a fantasy to be taken seriously. Others will
laugh at us if we dare admit that we seriously seek such
a lover. We want to deny this longing even to ourselves.
And yet we cannot. Not in the moments when finally
all the wrappings do become transparent or are swept
aside by some powerful current whose origin usually
alludes us. In these moments of truth, especially if we
dare stay with them for more than a fleeting painful
moment, we are confronted by the fact that in spite
of all our vaunted success and all our possessions and
even all our loves, in our deepest being we are aching
with longing. We are made for an infinite and an in-
finitely caring love, a love that will invade every depth
of our being and be there for us to embrace in an
all-satisfying love.

Human love is not enough. It is fallible. Even if it
has not yet failed us we know it can fail and most probably will fail us, and fail us again and again. Moreover,
no human love can penetrate deeply enough into us.
No matter how open we want to be, how vulnerably
we lay ourselves open, there still are those incommu-
nicable depths that we cannot bring forth and the other
cannot penetrate. We are left in our aloneness. And
we cannot ourselves enter as fully as we want into the
other. The most ardent human passion that leads us
to the most intimate of embraces in the end leaves us
the most lonely, for we know we have gone as far as
we can in communion and communication and yet we
remain apart.

We want more. We need more. Our deepest being cries for more. If there is no more, then we are the saddest joke around — the apex of creation and the ultimate frustration. No ... that cannot be. There must be something more. There must be a love and a lover that can fulfill us.

And there is. There is a love who is the very love of the Infinite, the embrace of the Infinite of the Infinite, that Kiss of the Father and the Son who is the Holy Spirit.

That there is such a Love and that that Love is ours can, in this life, be embraced only within the realms of faith. Happily, the Gospels give ample evidence of it. As he called Nathaniel, healed sinners, remonstrated with Peter, and in so many other instances, Jesus-God, Son of the Father, demonstrated that he knows what is within us. And yet, even with this knowledge, he gives us the ultimate proof of love: Greater love than this no one has than that one lay down one's life for a friend. Jesus-God, even while he knew all that is within us — all that sordidness and meanness we are so loath to admit even to ourselves — he freely, lovingly, and even eagerly laid down his life for us, to prove to us how much he loves us. And he abides with us, in his Church, in Sacrament, in each other, within our own hearts, and in his Word, to say to us again and again, in so many different ways: I love you. And he asks us, repeatedly, as he asked Peter: Do you love me? ... Do you love me more than these?

How do we come to know this love, to really know it, to know it experientially?

Through the Holy Spirit.

Jesus said to us at the Last Supper, when he opened his heart to us most fully: The Spirit, the Paraclete, will teach you all things.

The Holy Spirit comes to us to teach us in many different ways.

She can come in power, in wind and fire, shaking our whole world, instantly transforming our minds and hearts, enlightening and empowering us in new ways, as she came upon the apostles and disciples on that Pentecost, fifty days after Jesus' resurrection.

She can come when we least expect it and knock us off our high horse. Remember Saul the persecutor of Christ who became Paul the persecuted, readily suffering all for Christ. He rode toward Damascus on his high horse, burning with the zeal of the righteous. In a moment Jesus turned him into a humble disciple who knew his blindness and was willing to wait humbly to be enlightened in whatever way the Spirit should decide.

The Spirit can act in our lives in any way she chooses. However, God does not belie his own creation. God made us the pinnacle of his creation. He made us in his very own image. He gave us the power to love, even as he loves. He gave us freedom. And he respects that freedom totally. He will never invade our lives against our will. He humbly knocks.

What a beautiful scene the Lord presents in the Book of Revelation: Behold, I stand at the door and knock and *if* one opens I will come in and sit side by side with that one and sup. Two intimate friends enjoying a quiet meal together. And not sitting across the table from each other, but side by side — so we can press close together and even rest our heads upon his bosom, as did John, and hear the beating of his heart's love. Jesus-God wants the greatest possible and most fulfilling intimacy with us, as he opens to us the secrets of his love. Yet, he humbly knocks. He waits upon us. He will come in and share only if we open.

Do you remember the story of that great Italian artist who painted this scene from the Book of Revelation? His picture has Jesus standing at a big, strong door. Jesus appears as a pilgrim — a pilgrim of love. Gently he knocks, his eyes aglow with tender love. When the famous artist first exhibited his long-expected masterpiece there was much clucking of tongues. The master had messed up. He had missed a detail. There was Jesus standing at the door and there was obviously in this otherwise finely executed door no latch. The critics readily pointed out the missing element, lesser men all too happy to catch the master. The master smiled benignly through it all. No, he had not missed a detail. His critics had missed a detail — a most important detail of the revelation. There is no latch on Jesus' side of the door. This door, the door of our hearts, the door into our lives, can only be opened from the inside. We are and ever remain the masters of our God-given freedom. Behold, he, God, stands at the door of our hearts and humbly knocks.

If we are slow to open, he might press a bit further. In that passionate love song in which God seeks to describe for us something of his love for us, the Song of

Songs, God again appears at the door knocking. The Song tells how we hesitate, hold back, slow in our foolish self-content. The divine lover persists. He finds an opening in the lattice and eagerly reaches in. He touches us with the finger of his grace, seeking to stir our being. Still we remain free. We can arise and open. Or we can rest in our own doings, ignoring or trying to cover up with the pleasures of the night and the dreams of the deluded the deep longings of our own being.

We ever remain free. The Spirit came in fire and wind with power on Pentecost in response to the longings of the apostles and disciples and the mother in their midst. They had prayed. They had asked in faith. And she came.

Even the self-righteous Saul in his misguided zeal was truly seeking. He ran well but in the wrong direction. His good intentions were enough for the Divine Lover. The Lover came. And the hard-riding persecutor, because he was riding so hard, crashed into Love and fell to the ground. The enlightenment was too much for him. He could see nothing. He needed help — as do we all. And he freely decided to await it. He was given some days to sit in the darkness, experiencing his own blindness, so that he could freely choose to accept the enlightenment of baptism when it was offered to him.

God respects our freedom. The Spirit comes into our lives as the divinely effective teacher, who teaches not only by word but by work — if we want her. if we have an open and listening heart.

The Spirit speaks to us most powerfully when we

come together in the Christian assembly. When we manifest the Body of Christ that we are, when we incarnate it here and now, the Spirit, his Spirit becomes our Spirit, is present within us, in our midst, to speak to us and teach us all things, bringing effectively to mind all that he himself has taught us. The proclamation of Jesus' Gospel, his Good News, is a powerful moment. We shall speak of this more when we come to speak of the Mass.

The Spirit speaks to us through each other. Each of us has been baptized into Christ. Each of us is Christ in some real way. Through baptism we have been brought into a union with Christ that is beyond anything we can comprehend. We have a oneness that can be likened only to the union he has with his Father. And we know that that union is a oneness: one God though three divine persons. "I and the Father are one." Jesus and I are one. "Saul, Saul, why do you persecute me? . . . Whatever you do to the least of my brethren, you do to me." Jesus identifies himself with us who have been baptized into him. And he has given us his Spirit as our Spirit. The Spirit can speak and act through us, if we let her.

Some years ago I had the joy of spending some time with a saint. I was the guest of Mother Teresa of Calcutta in her home in that city. When I was about to take my leave I asked Mother to give me a word of life to take with me, to take back to my brothers at the monastery. I eagerly waited for the Spirit to speak to me through this most beautiful and open channel of her grace and light. Mother looked at me with those deep,

deep brown eyes that seem to invite one into the embrace of a most tender love. There was a pause. Mother seemed to be waiting for the Spirit to speak. Then, with careful articulation, the words came: "Tell them . . . to pray . . . that I DON'T GET IN GOD'S WAY."

The saints are the beautiful windows of Chartres, of the other great cathedrals, through which the divine light shines into our world, fully and beautifully revealing the caring love of our God. The rest of us are rather opaque, seeking, I hope, each day to become more translucent. The purer we are the more freely the Spirit can bring light to others through us. Let us more frequently have the courage to explicitly articulate the message of divine love in our speaking to one another. We need not be shy if we are humble, because we will realize that it is not our message but that of the Spirit who dwells within.

She can and did use Balaam's ass. If we ourselves are truly listening, the very being of each person and each thing speaks to us of divine love, for each is an expression of our God of love. The disharmonies may be many, the discordant noises we each introduce into our own lives. But the divine voice remains steady and clear deep within and is never fully drowned out for the one who has the ear to listen. Every person and everything they have to say to us in word or in action or in being can speak to us of divine love if we but have the heart to listen to the message of love.

There is one place where the Lord speaks to us in a most special and clear way. Using our human words the Lord speaks to us through persons divinely inspired to put down exactly what he wants to say to us. We have the privilege of being sons and daughters of the Book: the Bible we share with our Jewish sisters and brothers and the New Testament, where our Lord brings his revelation to a new fullness.

Our Bible is one of our most prized possessions. It is not a book to be left on the desk or put on the shelf with other books. It deserves to be enthroned in our homes, in our rooms, as a real presence, a place where, whenever we wish, we can encounter the living God and he will speak directly to us. In many churches today the Bible is not only enthroned but a lamp ever burns before it proclaiming this real presence.

As we come to our Lord present in his holy Scriptures to ask him to speak to us we want in some way to incarnate our sense of coming into his presence. This might be expressed in the reverence with which we take up the Sacred Text. We might want to go further and bow to the divine Presence before we take up the Text, or kneel or prostrate. We are coming into the presence of God. We might kiss the Sacred Text as something very precious.

At the same time we want to call upon the Holy Spirit to assist us in what we are about to enter into. As I have already mentioned, Jesus said the Spirit would be with us to teach us. And it was the Holy Spirit who inspired in a special way the writers of these texts so that what they contain is truly the Word of God. We ask the Spirit to make what is expressed within the Text come alive now in us.

A DIVINE COMMUNICATION

The communication, the teaching we are seeking when we come to the Lord in this way, is something that goes beyond human reason. We seek a divine communication that corresponds to the aspirations of our participated divine nature.

Let us explore this a little more deeply. Indeed, let's go all the way.

God the Father and God the Son and God the Holy Spirit, the three divine Persons, were ever deliriously happy in their love, communion, and union. Their love and their joy wanted to overflow. This is of the very nature of joy and happiness — it wants to be shared. In their joy, God made human beings to share in their joy.

Let me use a little analogy here that might bring out some aspects of the nature of this sharing. I once had a little dog, a purebred mongrel by the name of Diers. (How he got that name I have no idea.) Every morning we used to go for a walk. As I came out he would run up to me, jump up to give me a morning kiss — slobbering my beard. Then he would go bounding down the road, frequently looking back to be sure I was following. We became great friends. I enjoyed Diers and my time with him. But when I had some deep human joy I wanted to share, I did not go out to the dog house and sit down and say: Diers, guess what! No. When I had a joy to share I would seek out one of my brothers who could truly enter into my human joy. Such joy was beyond the capability of little Diers.

The fact is, though, that there is a greater distance between us and God than there is between me and Diers.

Now suppose my fairy godmother (it is always good to have a fairy godmother) came along and bopped little Diers on the head with her magic wand and, behold, Diers became human. Now Diers would be at my level of being. He would, of course, have to be endowed with human faculties to know and sense things as a human. Then he would be able to truly enter into my joy, to share my happiness.

What God did was not bop us on the head but dunk us in the water. We were baptized and made sharers of divine nature and life. We were raised up to the divine level of being. Still, in order to enter into the joy of the Lord, we need faculties that will enable us to know and sense things in a divine way. These also were given to us at baptism. We call them the gifts of the Holy Spirit: gifts because they are freely given; of the Holy Spirit because it is the Holy Spirit, who has become our spirit, who acts through them enabling us to function at the divine level, albeit still in the realm of faith as long as we are pilgrims on the way.

Through the gift of knowledge the Spirit gives us a sure sense of the divine in things. Through understanding she enables us to see what "stands under" — the Latin is *intellegere*, to "read within." We see through things and get a sense of their reality as it exists in God. The gift of wisdom — the Latin is *sapere*, to savor — enables us to taste and see how good the Lord is in all his works. Through the gift of counsel the Spirit moves us, without reasoning, to a sure sense of what course of action is right in the light of the revelation. It is precisely the activity of the Spirit through these gifts that we seek when we call upon her at the beginning of our encounter with God in the Sacred Scriptures. We ask the Spirit to take us beyond that to which our unaided human reason can attain, to bring us into the divine sense of things, to give us an experiential knowledge of God and what he wants to communicate to us. Our prayer is earnest indeed, for this is beyond us. Yet, it is what we truly long for, this experience of divine love and happiness and the guidance we need to live according to it, out of its fullness.

So we begin our encounter with God in his Revelation by coming into his presence, acknowledging the presence in some way that is significant to us and then most earnestly calling upon the Spirit to make this a time of divine communication.

LISTENING

We are now ready to settle down and *listen*. The word "reading" does not convey the attitude we want here. We are aware of Presence. We want the Lord to speak to us now through these his words, speak to us right where we are now on our journey, in our relationship with him. "Speak, Lord! Your servant — your disciple, your friend, your lover — wants to hear."

We listen attentively to each word, each phrase, each sentence. We listen to what is not said, what hides be-

tween the words. We are aware of the common teaching
of the Fathers, following the inspiration of Saint Paul,
that tells us that the words of Scripture have more
than one meaning. There is the *literal* meaning: this
is the basic sense of the words, the historical story, the
concrete teaching. This remains ever fundamental and
cannot be contradicted by the other senses. Then there
are the spiritual senses: the *allegorical* sense, or that
deeper meaning, appropriate to the communication
presently going on between the Lord and ourselves. It
translates the literal sense into "now." The *moral* sense
calls forth from me an appropriate response. And the
anagogical or *unitive* sense speaks to me of ultimate
meanings.

Let me give an example. Jerusalem is *literally* a city
on Mount Sion. *Allegorically*, Jerusalem is the Church.
Morally it calls forth from me that way of being and act-
ing that is appropriate to one who is Church, a member
of the Body of Christ. It is *ultimately* that heavenly
Jerusalem, the spotless bride that comes down from
above, the gathering of all the just.

When we are listening to the Lord we do not need
to be conscious of all these senses of Scripture. It is not
necessary to start analyzing the Text to seek to discern
them. It is enough to know that they are there and that
God can use any one of them at any time to speak to us.
We come to our listening with a certain simplicity. We
are with a most intimate Friend as well as a Master and
Teacher, our Lord and our God. Some days one dimension of our relationship with its attendant sentiments
stands out in our minds more than another. We are

simply there, letting the varied and rich relationship unfold. We want union and communion.

It is usually good to allow ourselves a set amount of time for this communication. We certainly do not want to try to get through a certain amount of matter: a page or paragraph or chapter. We listen. If the Lord speaks to us in the first words, we are content to remain with him in these. We let him take the lead. What we want is to allow him to communicate himself to us and bring us into the experience of himself and his experience of ourselves, of others, of the whole creation and of himself. We seek union.

It is easy to see how time can disappear in such a communion. Literally disappear, as we enter into God's NOW. When I say "a set amount of time," I mean a minimal amount of time. We want to set for ourselves a sort of "rule" that no matter how busy we are, no matter how full our lives are, we will each day give ourselves at least five or ten or fifteen minutes when we let go of everything else and sit with the Lord in this way. We have no hesitation, when our time permits, to prolong this very special time with our Friend, but, no matter what, we get our minimal time. Even when our mind seems intent on going elsewhere, we stay with the Text for the agreed amount of time. Even when our Lord seems to have gone elsewhere and the words wash over us like some meaningless collection of letters, we stay there, humbly waiting for the Lord to speak.

TAKE A WORD

When the Lord does "speak," when a word or phrase or sentence really communicates, we will not soon forget it. It stays with us as a word of life. We have all had the experience. Whether at the Eucharistic assembly or as a friend shared or in the course of our own listening, at times the Lord seems to actually speak a word to us. It makes a difference. It enlightens, strengthens, speaks of love and presence. These words are precious. They are the words that form in us the "mind of Christ."

But some days as we sit with the Scriptures, the Lord seems to remain silent — if not absent. Words, words and more words, but little real meaning for us now. At least not that deep experiential meaning that tells us of Presence. We long for it. What can we do?

We can take a word — a word, a sentence, or a phrase — and carry it with us. Maybe nothing seems to speak to us now. But as we move through the day with our chosen word, perhaps at some other moment when we least expect it, it will come alive and be just the word we need. Or maybe it will be the word someone else needs. And in the ministering to another we know the Presence. Carrying a word of the Lord with us throughout the day, perhaps sharing it, perhaps reflecting upon it, perhaps applying it, is bound to have a transforming influence on our lives and through us on the lives of those around us. We become ourselves little by little a revelation, a place where God reveals himself and his love to this world. A place where God's love turns up in this world.

Before we finish we want to be sure to thank the Lord. Isn't it wonderful! Any time we want we can sit down and the Lord himself will sit with us and speak to us personally. Is there any master as good as this Master? He loves us. He wants to be with us. He wants an intimate friendship with us. He is ready. He only awaits our opening, our desire, our welcoming. Thank you, Lord, for the gift of your Revelation and your Presence in that Revelation.

We best show our gratitude — lest it remain mere words — by living out of what he has given us.

LECTIO

This little practice we have described here, this personal meeting with the Lord in his Sacred Text, has traditionally been called *lectio* or *lectio divina* — divine reading. As I have said, "reading" does not really convey the attitude we want here. It is more a listening. Through the centuries, many of those who practiced *lectio* could not read. They depended more on their memories and what had been read to them. Or perhaps on frescoes, icons, and stained glass. *Lectio* is listening, receiving a word from the Lord — a living word from a present Lord.

The practice of *lectio* might be summed up thus:

We keep the Sacred Scriptures enthroned in our home in a place of honor as a real Presence of the Word in our midst.

1. Take the Sacred Text with reverence and call upon the Holy Spirit.

2. For five minutes (or longer, if you are so drawn) listen to the Lord speaking to you through the Text and respond to him.

3. At the end of the time, choose a word or phrase (perhaps one will have been "given" to you) to take with you and thank the Lord for being with you and speaking to you.

Traditionally, when we speak of *lectio* a whole process is invoked that can be summed up in four words: *lectio, meditatio, oratio,* and *contemplatio.*

Lectio is that listening of which we have already spoken. It is "reading" the Lord, receiving a word from him.

Meditatio: Today when we Christians speak of meditation we usually are thinking of a discursive process employing the mind and imagination, seeking to break through to the reality behind the thoughts and images. This is a relatively recent method. Meditation for some means transcendental meditation, a method seeking to empty the mind and come to an experience of the Absolute. In an earlier Christian tradition, meditation meant carrying the word received from *lectio* or from a spiritual mother or father. The word might be repeated in the mind or even on the lips. The aim was to let it form the heart — bring the mind down into the heart — and call forth a response.

Oratio was the particular response called forth by

the *meditatio*. As the word was allowed to form and shape the heart it might call forth a variety of responses: adoration, thanksgiving, petitions, repentance, and so forth.

Contemplatio is that complete and total "yes" to the Presence evoked by the word. We will come back to this in a later chapter.

For now, let us begin to listen: listen during a daily period of *lectio;* listen through the day to the word we take with us; listen to all the other expressions of divine Love in our lives. A regular practice of *lectio*, even for as little as five minutes a day, forms in us a listening heart, one attentive to the messages of love, and fills our life with an unexpected joy as we awaken to the God within.

CHAPTER TWO

DECADES OF ROSES

The rosary is a way of prayer that has long been a favorite among Catholics. Paradoxically, as its popularity or at least its use has begun to diminish among them it has begun to be popular among Christians of other communions. In these recent years we have been finding the freedom to receive of the riches that the Spirit has given to our separate communions during the centuries we have stood apart. We hope and we pray that these borrowings are stitches that are closing the wounds so that we can regain our lost unity.

The name "rosary" comes, of course, from rose. I suppose some other flower might have characterized these garlands of prayers. Nonetheless Scripture's "mystical rose" suggests itself. The deep red rose speaks of passion and blood. The white, white rose speaks of purity and birth. And yellow is the color of golden crowns. Joy, sorrow, glory, the rose is fitting for each.

The rosary may seem at first a rather complicated method of prayer. In fact it is quite simple. The fact that beads, whether they be stones or pebbles, seeds or knots, are found in almost all religious traditions, indicates that they are a natural help for prayer. They count the prayers we pray, they can measure the time, but most useful is the help they give us to center our attention. In the Christian tradition, though the symbolism of some numbers, especially three, is very strong, numbers in themselves have generally not been seen as very significant. The mystical numbers found in the inspired Scriptures called forth extensive commentaries on the part of the Fathers of the Church and some modern preachers follow in their footsteps, but these have not largely impacted on the lives of the average Christian. In prayer numbers are largely a means of expanding the time of prayer, while repetition serves either to deepen the impact of the chosen repetition or to occupy and quiet the thought processes so that the pray-er will be free to enter more deeply into communion with Reality.

THE DEVELOPMENT OF THE ROSARY

There are many ways in which we can pray the rosary. But first, let me very briefly recall the actual structure of this form of prayer as it has developed in the Christian tradition.

What we call today "the rosary" comes at the end of a long evolution. We know early Christians, notably the monks and recluses in the deserts, used piles of stones to number or prolong their prayer. The father would sit on the ground in front of his little cell or cave. Before him on the ground would be a pile of stones that he had collected and in all probability counted. As he prayed the "word" he had received from his spiritual father or had received in the course of his own listening to the Word of God, he moved one stone from the pile to begin another near it. "Lord, Jesus Christ, Son of the living God, have mercy on me, the sinner." As he repeated his prayer a second time, he moved another stone. Little by little the first pile diminished and the second grew. His time of prayer or a designated part of it came to an end as the last stone was transferred to the new pile.

The piles kept the pray-er in place. This had its advantages, furthering stability even as it engaged the body. The spirit was the freer. But such stability could have its disadvantages as well. If an aching stiffness did not creep into the muscles, a drowsiness might well creep into the attention. It was natural enough to devise a way in which one could transfer some of the benefits of the stones to a more mobile possibility. The fathers often wove baskets and rope — another way of counting prayers or timing prayer, as well as supporting the needs of the body; they could easily weave string and tie knots. They could also thread seeds. Fifty, a hundred, or thirty-three — the years of Jesus' life and a third of a hundred — or three hundred: no number was sacrosanct, many were used. The multiples could be many as one pushed toward continuous prayer. I can recall seeing a cord of a hundred beads that had three pendants of ten beads each. As the pray-er completed a circle he moved a bead on the first pendant. When these ten were moved and he had said the prayer a thousand times, a bead was moved on the second pendant. When the ten beads on the second pendant were moved (and he had said the prayer ten thousand times) a bead on the third pendant was moved. When the final bead on this third pendant was moved he would have prayed his prayer one hundred thousand times!

In 525 Saint Benedict of Nursia wrote a Rule for Monasteries that in time became the common rule for monks in all parts of western Europe. One of the basic practices he called his monks to was the regular recitation of the 150 psalms of the Psalter. The monks usually completed each psalm with a doxology. The monks were expected, in the course of their first months in the monastery, to commit the 150 psalms to memory. This ill-suited simpler folks and, indeed, the recitation of the psalms, since some of them are quite long, demands more time than most could give. Long hours for prayer were the luxury of monks and nuns. Yet those who worked about the monastery and other pious folk wanted to be united to the prayer of the monks. Hence there grew up the practice of praying 150 Paters or Paters and Glorias — "Our Fathers" and doxologies. A string of beads was aptly used to count these. It might have a full 150 beads or it might have 50, with the expectation one would go around it three times.

While the monks repeated the psalms they did not

necessarily ponder the very familiar words they were repeating. Especially on feasts they wanted to think about or contemplate the mystery they were celebrating. At other times, such as during Lent or Advent, they would turn their attention to the season and its deeper meanings. To aid them in this, the cantor or one of the monks or perhaps all the monks would sing, before they began the psalm, a short piece, called an antiphon, which would tersely express some facet of the feast or season.

The monks, in their devotion to Mary, whom they honored as the mother of their Lord, developed a "little office," which was usually prayed before the principal or "divine office" laid out by Saint Benedict, following the living tradition of the Church. The antiphons of this little office brought to mind the events in the life of the Blessed Virgin.

In imitation of this the simple folks began to pray, along with the 150 Paters, another 150 Aves or "Hail, Marys" — a prayer made up of the salutation of the angel Gabriel to Mary at the moment of the annunciation and the salutation of Mary's cousin Elizabeth, when Mary went to visit her: *Hail, Mary, full of grace. The Lord is with you. Blessed are you among women and blessed is the fruit of your womb.* Later, the holy name of Jesus was added. And still later a petition: *Holy Mary, Mother of God, pray for us sinners, now and at the hour of our death.*

As the common folks prayed their Aves, they, too, were invited to reflect on the events of Mary's life. And terse phrases, usually drawn from Scriptures, were added to the Aves. To add 150 Scripture texts to the 150 Aves was a bit much. We find them in some manuscripts — and today they are found in booklets called *The Scriptural Rosary* — but how much they came into widespread practice is questionable. Soon enough they were reduced to more general reflections on the major events of Mary's life, fifteen of them, one for each "decade" or ten Hail Marys. The ten Hail Marys came to be marked off with a Pater at the beginning and a doxology at the end. And thus we came to the present form of our rosary: fifteen decades, each with an Our Father, ten Hail Marys, and a doxology, and with a particular event or "mystery" in the life of Mary assigned to it for meditation or contemplation. A pendant before, with four beads — an Our Father and three Hail Marys — provides a preparation, which is used in various ways to prepare for the rosary. Saint Benedict had told his monks: Whenever you begin a good work pray most earnestly that the Lord will help you to bring it to perfection. A crucifix at the end of the pendant is usual as is a medal of some sort where the decades join the pendant.

PRAYING THE ROSARY

When praying the beads, commonly we make the sign of the cross over ourselves with the crucifix — from forehead to heart, from left shoulder to right — praying: *In the name of the Father and of the Son and of the Holy Spirit. Amen.* The Apostles' Creed is then usually professed, inviting us to enter more deeply into the realm of faith.

The preparatory Our Father and Hail Marys may be a prayer for help to pray well. "We do not know how to pray as we ought, but the Holy Spirit prays in us." We need help to pray well. Some go further in their precision and pray the three Aves specifically for an increase of faith, hope, and love. Let each use them as best helps.

There are different ways in which we may pray the decades.

We may want simply to pray the prayers. There is no fuller, more powerful, or more holy prayer than the Lord's Prayer. To make each phrase of it our own prayer, more deeply ours through the repetition, is a very good way to pray. Saints have written books on the Lord's Prayer, the fruit of their own repetitive praying of it. It can form our mind and heart to perfect sanctity, that is, to perfect oneness with the mind and heart of Christ. We have in this prayer the most fundamental attitudes proper to the one who has been baptized into Christ.

To say, again and again, *Hail, Mary... Hail, Mary... Hail, Mary...* can delight the heart of one who loves. It joins us with an angelic salutation. It leads us more deeply into the mystery of the incarnation. *Holy Mary, pray for us... sinners...* puts us more in touch with our need, our reality, and it gives us the hope and consolation of a mother's caring. After this it usually takes no effort on our part to enter into the prostration of the doxology.

The constant humble repetition of these prayers,

aided by the beads that support our attention and our
continuance, can take us, under the graceful action of
the Holy Spirit, more and more deeply into the reality
of who God is, who we are, and who Mary is in relation
to God and to us. It is all there. We do not have to go
beyond the words of the customary prayers — prayers
that are drawn from the inspired Scriptures.

Such simplicity in prayer is exquisite. And it is only
the most gifted ones, simple and pure, who can remain
constantly faithful to it. Just as the Church invites us
to enriching variety through the celebration of seasons
and feasts, so the decades, one after the other, invite us
to be enriched with different events or mysteries within
the life of Jesus and Mary.

We can enter into these with the Aves as a quiet
background of prayer.

We can pause at the beginning of each decade, before
or after the Pater, not only to announce the mystery,
but to reflect upon it. In a group this can take the form
of a group meditation. I recall a beautiful experience I
had one evening in the home of a friend with a large
family. We were all gathered around the supper table,
settling quietly at the end of a very fine meal. At this
point the youngest, Chris, brought a humidor from the
sideboard. From it each drew out a rosary. Then Maureen, probably twelve at the time, started us off. We
made the sign of the cross and Maureen went on to
announce: This evening we are going to meditate on
the second joyful mystery, the visitation. She went on
to share some of her thoughts about Mary's journey
to the hill country. Soon others joined in. After a good

fifteen minutes of sharing, Maureen led us in praying the Our Father, the ten Hail Marys, and the doxology. We ended with the hymn with which it is quite traditional to end the rosary, the Salve, Regina — Hail, Holy Queen.... This family prayed only one decade of the rosary each evening, but they gave a good bit of time to it and truly entered, as a family, into the mystery prayed. We can all exercise such freedom in using this means of prayer the Church and our Christian tradition offer us. It is a means and it is to be used in the way in which it best serves us, bringing us to the end it is meant to serve.

Rather than pausing at the beginning of the decade to reflect upon the mystery, we might go right on with the prayers, but as we pray them, with mind and imagination we might explore the mystery, seeking one way or another to enter into it.

We may, as it were, be outside the scene, looking in. What we are beholding is in fact one of the great dramatic moments in the history of our human family. It is a significant moment in the lives of some persons whom we very much love: Jesus, Mary, her husband, Joseph, other friends. The event, with its evolving scenes, has a lot to say to us. We can let it speak to us again and again, ever more deeply.

Or we might, as it were, step into the scene, and play one of the roles: an onlooker at the time, a humble donkey or one of the main players, even Mary or Jesus himself. Day after day, as we pray in this way we can get new and very different perspectives upon what is taking place. How did Jesus experience this event? How did

Mary? What did it say to the curious onlooker..., to the seeker..., to one who really cared? To the enemy? Is there any limit to the number of ways in which we might enter into the mysteries of the rosary? This is perhaps why some old folks, with the freedom of old age, can spend all the hours of the day with the beads in their hands.

However, I suspect at that point in life, the way one prays the mysteries has come to a greater simplicity. We may not need to wait till old age, though, before we begin to enjoy a more contemplative way of praying the rosary. As we finger the beads we can just rest in the reality of the respective mystery. No imaginings, no thoughts, just resting in the reality — a truly refreshing resting, one that deepens and enlivens faith and hope and love.

In any one of these approaches to the mysteries our attention can be primarily on the historic event, which is indeed present to us now as living in the eternal "now" of God. What is happening and what that says to us in our present moment in our own personal appropriation of salvation history may well be what is uppermost. But we can — it is another legitimate way to approach the mysteries of the rosary — ponder more the particular virtues we see at play in the event we are meditating upon. In each mystery there are many virtues present. Let us, by way of example, look at the visitation. What faith Mary shows, setting out on that long journey on the word of God's messenger. There is no question in her mind. He has spoken and she is off. What courage, what fortitude. This is a young woman, who is just beginning her first pregnancy, with all the questions and fears that surround a first pregnancy, and yet she sets off to a distant place, knowing she will have a return journey to make when she is even further into her mysterious pregnancy. She steps out from home and family and relies on whom? Faith, courage, love. . . . It was loving concern for her cousin that sent her forth. How much easier it would have been to stay at home. Others could care for the old woman. But could anyone else understand the mystery of her cousin's pregnancy like Mary? And so we ponder the virtues the mystery exemplifies.

There come times though when we can not tolerate any more words or thoughts. Perhaps we are sick, or very tired, or too full — too full with one emotion or another. At such times we might just want to hold our rosary in hand and in some way let it mutely pray for us, let our holding it be a cry to Mary for help, let it be a chain that binds us with heaven when all we can do is hang on. Is this a legitimate way to use the rosary? Maybe it is not a way to "say" the rosary, but it certainly is a way to "pray" the rosary. And that is what the rosary is all about: prayer.

I think most of us Catholics want the rosary in our hands when we are laid in a coffin. And we want it in our hands in the moments that come before that, in that "hour of our death" about which we prayed so continuously as we prayed the rosary. Even if in no conscious way we can then pray, they are our beads and God sees them in our hands and they are our prayer.

THE FIFTEEN MYSTERIES

As we have mentioned above, the rosary is a method of prayer that evolved over the centuries. Today, when we speak of the mysteries of the rosary, we are readily understood to refer to fifteen generally accepted mysteries. These have been the commonly accepted fifteen mysteries of the rosary for over four or five centuries now. There are other forms of praying with beads: the Franciscan Crown, the Rosary of the Seven Sorrows, the Bridgettines Rosary, etc. When we speak of one of these others we are usually quite specific. When we speak simply of the "rosary," we usually mean our chaplet of decades, five or fifteen, which are used to pray with these fifteen mysteries:

The Five Joyful Mysteries

The First Joyful Mystery: The Annunciation

The Second Joyful Mystery: The Visitation

The Third Joyful Mystery: The Nativity of Jesus

The Fourth Joyful Mystery: The Presentation of Jesus in the Temple

The Fifth Joyful Mystery: The Finding of Young Jesus in the Temple

The Five Sorrowful Mysteries

The First Sorrowful Mystery: Agony and Consolation

The Second Sorrowful Mystery: Jesus Is Scourged

The Third Sorrowful Mystery: Jesus Is Crowned with Thorns

The Fourth Sorrowful Mystery: Jesus Carries His Cross

The Fifth Sorrowful Mystery: The Crucifixion

The Five Glorious Mysteries

The First Glorious Mystery: The Resurrection

The Second Glorious Mystery: The Ascension

The Third Glorious Mystery: The Descent of the Holy Spirit upon the Apostles

The Fourth Glorious Mystery: The Assumption of the Blessed Virgin Mary

The Fifth Glorious Mystery: The Coronation of the Blessed Virgin Mary

These are the basic mysteries or events in the lives of Jesus and Mary that invite us to enter into ever deeper communion with our Savior and his mother. There is more than enough here to keep us going for a lifetime. Indeed, we will spend an eternity — whatever that means — in wonderment at these events of salvation history.

OTHER MYSTERIES TO BE PONDERED

Yet our bishops have invited us to expand our considerations if we wish. They have pointed out how this very

traditional selection takes a leap from the boyhood of
Jesus, or his coming into manhood, to the beginning of
his passion. The whole of his public ministry as well as
many years of his hidden life are passed over. We can
most fruitfully pause at one event after the other from
this long period and make it our focus as we pray our
decades.

I have explored the possibilities this opens up in
other writings and I don't intend to do that again here.
In an appendix I will offer some suggestive quintads for
your possible use. What I would like to develop here is
the link between the rosary and what we have spoken
about in our first chapter, *lectio divina*.

THE ROSARY AND *LECTIO DIVINA*

In our daily *lectio* we seek to be open and totally recep-
tive so that the Lord can give us a word of life for the
day—our daily bread. I have suggested that this word
of life is not only for the moment of *lectio* but that it is
well to consider it our daily bread, our bite, our nourishment for the day, something to be carried with us
through the day, letting it open out more and more as
we experience it in other contexts, letting it open out
those other contexts by the light it brings to them.

Our daily *lectio* and our daily rosary can be integrated in this wise: The word that we have received at
our *lectio* can be the word that we ponder as we pray
our decades. This, of course, can be done in different
ways also.

We can ponder the appropriate mysteries, letting the word we have received shed its particular light on them. Perhaps you can remember seeing a store window with a magical winter scene. In front of the light that illumines it is a revolving disc with transparencies of different colors. First the whole scene is bathed in green, then in yellow, then in red, then in blue. With each revolution the scene is so transformed that we can hardly tire from looking at it. Each day's word can so transform the familiar events of the rosary.

Another possibility, no doubt more complicated, would be this. To ponder in the first decade on the word we have received today. In the second, the word we received yesterday. And so on back through the words of the past days. So often the words that give us so much light and consolation in our daily *lectio* are quickly lost. This is not necessarily a tragedy. The Lord gives us our *daily* bread. Nonetheless a storehouse of this bread that comes down from heaven can be useful and life-giving. Those who have studied the workings of the human memory have noted that if we recall something within a short time of our first encountering it and then twenty-four hours later and then from time to time during the succeeding days, it will become ours forever. By bringing back the fruit of our daily *lectio* through our daily rosary we can possess it more permanently as an ongoing source of nourishment. But we do not want to use this merely as a memory technique. Certainly not. Bringing the word repeatedly to prayer enables the Lord to open it out more and more for us. Also, it allows that word and our experience of

it to become more and more integrated into our consciousness, more effectively forming in us the mind of
Christ.

A GIFT FROM HEAVEN

The rosary is in itself a very simple method of prayer.
It grew up in the Christian tradition to respond to the
need of simple people who wanted to be in union with
the prayer of the Church, entering ever more fully into
who they were as persons of the Church: members of
the whole Christ. The rosary responded to that aspi-
ration so well that in Catholic mythology it is often
presented as a gift from heaven, Mary herself handing
it to Saint Dominic. It certainly is a gift of heaven itself, given in the way most of heaven's gifts are given:
in and through us.

The rosary is a very simple way of prayer, yet it is
one that can be used in very many ways, as we have
seen. It is important for us, because of the richness of
its potential, not to lose its simplicity and to keep its
real purpose as a means ever in view. The false self can
very easily turn it into our project, producing an ever
richer array of thoughts and experiences. The rosary is
a means, a means given to us. We are free to use it as
much and as little as we wish, in any and in as many
ways as we wish. But we would be foolish if we used it
for any other end than to come to a fuller realization of
who we "be" — to awaken to the God within.

Like all the gifts of heaven, we can grossly fail to appreciate what we have been given. We can settle for the rosary being so much less in our lives than it can be. At the same time it is one gift of an enormous plethora that comes to us from the divine bounty. We do not need to use, we cannot use, all that comes to us, for the bounty is beyond our receptivity. It is good to know that the rosary is there for us. It comes most highly endorsed. It has been used by saints and helped to make them saints. We can freely use it in our coming to sainthood, in our coming to be who we are. And we can freely lay it aside when we don't need it, when other gifts are serving us better, when life is full of the divine. And we can use it when life is full of the divine to help us abide in that reality. We best show our appreciation for a gift when we use it in the way that best benefits us in accord with who we are and where we are. This is the freedom of the children of God.

CHAPTER THREE

WALKING IN HIS WAY

A myth is a fabrication that conveys to us a more obscure and often times transcendent reality. The myth itself may be purely a fabrication brought into being for the purpose of this representation or it may be an actual historical reality created by God that is nonetheless used to point to another reality. For example, Jesus' ascension is a historical reality, yet it points to the ultimate meaning of his life and the transcendence to which we are all called. Myth often conveys reality more fully and more powerfully than a bald recitation of historical fact. According to myth, frequently portrayed in sculpture and painting, the Virgin Mother gave the rosary directly to Saint Dominic. The rosary is, indeed, a gift of heaven given to us through the Virgin Mary though in fact the human agency employed by God may obscure our perception of the directness of the gift.

The myth that the Way of the Cross, or the stations, originate with the Blessed Virgin may be closer to historical reality. It is easy to imagine that after Jesus rose from the dead and ascended to heaven, Mary would have retraced the steps of that fateful day that had engraved itself deep within her maternal being, seeking again at the end the empty tomb. Her Son, in a sense, was gone from her. To this extent his death had a certain finality. But the whole of his horrible death was illuminated by the fact that it led to what was now an empty tomb. Mary, who was used to pondering all things in her heart, must have pondered deeply the mystery of suffering, seeking to understand or at least in some way to enter into the mystery of why her beloved Son's most loving Father demanded such a price of him — and her.

WITH MARY

To make the Stations of the Cross with Mary is undoubtedly one of the most gripping ways in which we can tread this path of suffering and triumphant love. Mary invites us to enter most intimately into the pathos of a beautiful young man being destroyed, and that most brutally, by the jealous machinations of politically ambitious religious leaders who were so completely betraying their sacred trust. Every virtue in Mary must have seemed to have been mocked by the injustice being perpetrated here: her deep love of God and man and of the God-Man, her faith and hope, her profound compassion toward all human suffering, her piety as a devout Jew awaiting and longing for the Messiah, her sense of justice, and her virginal modesty and sensitive chastity as she saw this Man displayed naked on the cross. The movements in the soul of Mary as she lived and relived this Way of the Cross invite us to grow as truly human and compassionate persons. Yes, to walk to Calvary with Mary is a school of love beyond any other left to us save that of walking in her son, Christ Jesus, who was her model and her source.

THE VIA DOLOROSA

Whenever I think of the Stations of the Cross, there comes to my mind the picture of Pope Paul VI engulfed in a crushing mob in the streets of Old Jerusalem. When that picture was first flashed across the television screens of the world and reproduced on the pages of thousands of newspapers and magazines we were not yet used to seeing a pope traveling abroad. Paul VI, who pioneered true renewal in the Catholic Church in many ways, was the first pontiff really to break out of the prison of the Vatican in modern times. Quite fittingly one of his first journeys was to his Master's own country. As he trod in the saving steps of his Lord, whose vicar he was, police, security guards and government officials tried hard to protect him. But this was all but impossible in those narrow, always crowded streets of Old Jerusalem. The crush of people was great and at times seemed to threaten to totally crush the diminu-

tive figure in white. Yet through it all he preserved a
profound serenity and an inwardness that bespoke a
deep communion with the One in whose steps he then
trod.

To make the Stations of the Cross through the
streets of Jerusalem is a very special experience. Few,
I suspect, succeed in maintaining the same constant
equanimity and recollection that marked the Pontiff.
Of itself it is a crushing, confusing, distracting experience. Yet there is something actual in all of this. Was
this not the way it was the first time this path was
followed by the Son of Man himself? Life in Jerusalem did not stop, especially on that eve of the great
Passover, simply because some "malefactors" were being led out to execution. That was much the Romans'
business, though the Jewish leaders did seem to be in-
volved in this one, and the victim was someone rather
special. Was another true prophet being treated in the
way God's chosen usually treated his prophets? Still life
goes on. The preparations for the all-important Seder
must be completed. There was shopping to do and a
lamb to be sacrificed, a house to be especially cleaned
and a table to be set. Life went on even as Life went
to death.

THE STATIONS TODAY

Every Friday afternoon at about three o'clock a brown-
robed friar with a portable speaker gathers together the
faithful in the courtyard of the Muslim school that

abuts the Temple precincts. Through an arch on one side of the courtyard one gets one of the best overall views of the vast Temple area, which on Friday, the holiday of the followers of Mohammed, is closed to the public. The school is also closed. It is one of the clauses of the very complex agreement defining the rights of the three major faiths in this thrice-holy city that allows the Catholics to gather here on Friday afternoon at three to begin the Way of the Cross. This is the traditional site of the Antonianum, the Roman fortress in whose forecourt Jesus was condemned to death.

After commemorating Jesus' condemnation the procession descends the steep steps to the wall in front of the Church of the Flagellation. Here the cross was placed upon Jesus' already sorely bruised shoulders. And the long journey to Calvary began — long not in distance but in the duration of the sufferings of a Man. The Sisters of Sion have a large convent on the right side of the road here that goes by the address: The Second Station of the Cross. They have done some remarkable excavating beneath their house. It is now possible to descend and walk on the very stones on which Jesus and his contemporaries trod that Friday we now call "Good." They have also restored a Roman arch of triumph and have enthroned the Blessed Sacrament beneath it for perpetual adoration. In the end it is the condemned Galilean who is the Victor.

Jesus was not able to go very far — he had been abused all through the night and ferociously beaten — before the weight of the cross overcame him and he fell to the ground: the third station. We are at the corner of the road, just a few hundred yards from where we began. At many of the stations there are small chapels, which are usually open only on Friday afternoon. Each one is hardly more than a "hole in the wall," but each is distinctive and bespeaks a long tradition. Because they are so small, no attempt is made to enter. The procession remains outside while the friar leads in a meditation and some prayers.

The fourth-station chapel, a few hundred feet around the corner — we are now on what is called the Via Dolorosa — is one of the largest. Over the door there is a bas-relief depicting Jesus' encounter with his mother. One wonders if this were not the most painful moment for Jesus in the whole of this sad journey: Son, behold your mother.

As the procession — if it can be called that; it is more like a motley crowd — wends its way slowly down the Via Dolorosa, one station follows the other.

The woman whom tradition calls Veronica — *vera icona*, the true icon, for that is what she is said to have taken away on her cloth — pushes her way through a similar crowd and the burly Roman guards to perform a courageous act of mercy. How the salty sweat must have burned his eyes and his many open wounds. The respite was momentary but the kindness embraced the heart.

This Man was like us in all things — but sin. The long brutal vigil, the loss of blood, the heat of the day, not to speak of the psychological agonies, were taking their toll. Their victim would not last to complete his agony on his assigned cross. Something must be done. Enter a man whom tradition has evaluated in very diverse ways. Was the passerby a total stranger, a most unwilling helper? Or was he a disciple who had dared to follow and seized a chance to be near and help? Did he begin as a stranger and end as a disciple? Two of the early Christians, Alexander and Rufus, proudly claimed him: Our father Simon helped Jesus carry his cross. Whoever he was, whatever be his story, whether he knew it or not, he was a most privileged person. Through the ages he has been the stand-in for the millions who have wanted to help Jesus carry his cross and fill up what is wanting in the passion of Christ.

The help was not enough. Again Jesus crumpled and fell to the ground. Weak, torn, bruised in every part, how agonizing must a fall have been. And the rising. We reflect on some of our own cuts and bruises and begin to calculate. But our calculations do not take us very far. We have never known anything like this. He goes on — for us.

Compassion is again present in the presence of women (where are the men?). Yet his is the greater compassion. Can you imagine being in such sore straits as he and yet being intent on the compassionate sorrow of others — a suffering so minuscule compared to his own. Yet, with prophetic insight he saw what lay ahead for the unfaithful city. It would be horrible enough. His words and his love would still be there then, but then as now there would be few enough who would avail themselves of it and its healing power. He loved children. His heart was torn, just like his body, at the thought of what these little ones, now before him, would one day

suffer. How he would have liked to lay down his burden
for just a minute or two and embrace and bless them:
suffer the little ones to come unto me and forbid them
not.

At this point in our journey the procession veers off
to the right. We are approaching Calvary. It is now, as
it long has been, fully within the city. There is much
built upon it. The devotion of centuries has put up
chapel and church and basilica, and even a monastery
on the roof of the basilica, while Muslims made more
pragmatic use of the spaces they could find. It is a jum-
ble. But before we attempt to ascend, we stop at a spot
marked on a wall, traditionally the place of Jesus' third
fall. He must have been flat out this time. Would he
ever make it up the short but sharp incline? Was he
more dragged than helped as he stumbled along? O
holy Victim!

We retrace our steps to the Via Dolorosa, then up
an incline and some steps, then through a passage and
on till we reach the door of the basilica. Once in we
mount the last steep ascent to the top of Calvary. Here
he was stripped, thrown down upon the rough wood,
and nailed. (A Roman Catholic altar now marks the
spot.) A few words say it. It did not take much time. It
was an agony far beyond anything most of us will ever
know or come near conceiving.

Then the cross is raised. (A Greek Orthodox altar
marks the spot. Beneath the altar one can reach down
and touch the native stone. This rise called Golgotha
was at the edge of a quarry. On the back of it are in-
scriptions from the first century, before the destruction

of the city, which give witness to the earliest cult.) At times this small sanctuary is very crowded, as at the moment of the completion of the Stations. Other times it is a very silent and darksome place where silent adorers enter into deepest communion with the Victim of Calvary. One thing is certain: words will never be adequate for what has taken place here. The friar leads the meditation in the usual way with the customary prayers, but there is something deeper going on in the minds and hearts of each participant. The words but provide the space for communion.

The procession crowd stumbles down the very steep steps, back to the plane of the basilica. Here is the anointing stone. We recall that moment, past death, when a most sacred body, now deprived of its life-giving soul, was hastily prepared for the grave. It is the place of the Pietà, but Michelangelo's masterpiece seems profane in comparison to the ancient somber space of the anointing stone, resting eerily in the uneven light of the surrounding oil lamps. One senses very deeply something is coming to an end.

The tomb is only thirty-three steps away. The architectural activities of the ages have isolated it. It is an almost garish cube, but the soot of a multitude of lamps burning for a multitude of centuries has mellowed it into a burnished temple. Within all is prayer. It is almost necessary to crawl to get within. Marble, silver, gold, artwork cover all. But there is something more here. There is a sacred emptiness. The stations cannot end with a burial. The tomb stands at the axis of this great sanctuary — empty. Yes, he was buried. But

not for long. There is nothing here that inclines us to
stay long with the thought of burial. Everything points
to resurrection. Christ is risen! That is the reality that
gives the whole journey its meaning. If Christ be not
risen our faith is in vain. Everything is in vain. But the
tomb is empty, Christ is risen. And now everything has
meaning. Alleluia!

THROUGH THE CENTURIES

Not one stone was left standing on another. The destruction of Jerusalem was almost as total as anything
could be. There were a few stones that escaped. They
are now prized as a "wailing wall." It is deeply touching
to stand by this wall and pray. Jesus' eyes had looked
upon it. It was part of the sacred precinct, his Father's
house, which his flaring anger sought to reclaim for
the All-Holy. Centuries lapsed between the time the
mother of Jesus trod the Via Dolorosa and another
mother sought to refind it.

In the fourth century after the coming of Christ,
Constantine's mother, Helena, made the quest of the
cross of Christ her particular concern. At the same time
the Via Dolorosa was traced out and pious pilgrims
began to follow it in prayerful memory. When they
returned home they talked about the experience and
wrote about it. For a few centuries pilgrims followed
after pilgrims, seeking the Holy City, seeking the Way
of the Cross, seeking the Hill of the Skull. Then once
again their way was blocked as new conquerors took

control of the area. Again centuries lapsed and crusades were mounted. Devotion to the Holy Land and to the sacred places there grew. The city was finally freed and pilgrims again went there, though often in peril of their lives.

Not too many of God's poor could ever hope to make the long journey from Europe to undertake the short journey to Calvary. Devotion brought it to them. Stations were erected at European shrines; then in parish churches and cathedrals, then up the sides of mountains and through forests. They could be found everywhere in Christendom. Even till today. There are not many churches that do not have a Way of the Cross, if not in the main nave, then somewhere within the domain.

Still there were those who could not make even this small journey; the crippled, the sick, the bedridden. For them crucifixes were prepared and specially blessed. Holding the cross in hand, mentally they trace the Savior's footsteps and meditate on the fourteen events; it is as if they traverse the streets of Jerusalem.

It was very early in the popularization and dissemination of this devotion that the fourteen stations we have described were established:

1. Jesus is condemned to death.

2. Jesus takes up his cross.

3. Jesus falls for the first time.

4. Jesus meets his mother.

5. Veronica wipes Jesus' face.

6. Simon helps Jesus carry his cross.

7. Jesus falls the second time.

8. Jesus consoles the sorrowing women.

9. Jesus falls the third time.

10. Jesus is stripped of his garments.

11. Jesus is nailed to the cross.

12. Jesus dies on the cross.

13. Jesus is taken down from the cross.

14. Jesus is laid in the tomb.

As we pray the Stations of the Cross, we are expected to walk from one station to the next, symbolically making the journey along the Via Dolorosa in Old Jerusalem. The Stations should be set up, at least a wooden cross at each station, with some space from station to station. In a communal celebration, especially if there is a large crowd and space is limited, it is enough if the leader and perhaps a few with him make the journey in the place of all the participants. Often times at each station the event to be meditated upon is depicted in some way: wood, stone, glass, paint, print. In some countries, especially during Holy Week, living persons reenact Christ's journey as part of a communal celebration. Tastes certainly vary here, as does what helps true prayer. The way we meditate on the Stations can also vary much. Some will find it helpful to give the imagination full play and let it call forth deep emotions leading to deeply felt prayer. Others will prefer something simpler. As with the rosary we can actually enter within the scene and be a present spectator and even a participant. We can walk close to Mary or John or struggle with Simon the Cyrene. We can be conscious of our oneness with Christ. When we are suffering much ourselves this is often the most meaningful way to walk the Via Dolorosa. Our compassion can go beyond words or images and just simply be. That is enough. We can ponder in the heart: let the reality rest in our hearts till it forms our hearts and draws us beyond ourselves into the inexpressible depths of this mystery of love. Throughout let us never forget that the events we are pondering are living realities now in the NOW of God and that the person who is living this Way of the Cross is living within us now. We are not harking back to the past. We are making the ultimate moments of the creation present in our lives right now. It is within this reality that we come to really know, to experientially know the compassion of our Lord and Savior Jesus Christ. The God-Friend-Lover who dwells within is the one who loves us this much. Greater love than this no one has than to lay down one's life for another. We are the other for whom he lays down his life, lays it down with such graphic brutality to claw our well-sealed hearts open. The Stations are powerful prayer to soften hard hearts, to water dry hearts, to warm cold hearts — to make hearts hearts again.

A NEW STATION

Where sin abounds, grace abounds yet more. Maybe that is the reason why in our time there has blossomed a penetrating sense of the central reality of our faith: He is risen. So powerful has this sense become in some that it has not been possible to leave the crucified Lord as the dominant image, central in our churches. The glorious risen Christ has appeared above our altars. We are an Easter people.

And the Stations cannot end with a sealed tomb. That is not the reality. The tomb at Jerusalem is open and empty and made as glorious as artisans of the different ages have been able to make it. Christ is risen. A fifteenth station has been added. We go forth from our sorrowful journey knowing that our sorrow has borne fruit. If we have died with Christ, and that means dying to our selfish sinfulness, we have risen with Christ. We live in hope and expectation.

This fifteenth station speaks to us of the dignity, the sublimity, the destiny of the human person. Yes, we all face death. But this horrible tearing apart of the human person is not the end. It is but an interlude, a moment when sin thinks it has the victory only to find a greater victory lies in wait for those who belong to Christ. We shall rise again and be one with him in his glory because of this journey we call the Way of the Cross, which is in some way being lived out in the lives of each of us as a member of Christ.

We are, though, missing something very important if we see the fifteenth station only in its eschatological meaning. Yes, it is ultimately most important that we will all rise again and be with Christ in glory. But Christ has risen and begun to reign. The fruits of his passion and death are already alive among us. Human dignity is reaffirmed. The fifteenth station speaks to us and sends us forth now to live in our dignity as men and women risen with Christ and to do all that we can to make it possible for every other person to live in that dignity. The reign of Christ has begun. Those who are one with him and who are his followers seek to make his kingdom come now, to do his will on earth even as it is done in heaven. We reverence every human person as well as the environment, which should be worthy of the sons and daughters of God. And we seek to express our reverence effectively in working for the dignity of each. We should not rest content as long as any human person is forced to live in a subhuman way that is unworthy of his or her dignity as one who has risen in Christ.

The fifteenth station is not only a celebration of victory. It is a mandate.

BIBLICAL STATIONS
OF THE CROSS

Another great grace of our times has been the renaissance of biblical studies. Happily and necessarily this grace has not been restricted to academia. It has more than trickled down to the everyday life of the Church. Indeed, it has been a real leaven, enlivening the whole.

Every aspect of our Christian life is being reexamined and renewed in the light of scriptural insight. We cannot thank the Lord enough for this. This seems to be a grace that he wanted to give us four centuries ago. But the old wineskins were too dried out and burst asunder. Now at last there are fresh skins, expanding and world-embracing. And the new wine is inviting us all to a new celebration of life.

As we have already seen, this renewed sense of the fullness of the Scriptures has invited us to enlarge greatly our repertoire of mysteries to be meditated upon as we pray the rosary. It has also reached out toward the way in which some pray the Stations of the Cross. A new series of fourteen stations has come into use. This series has received a certain implicit approbation in that it was used by Pope John Paul II on Good Friday in 1991. It more widely embraces the passion and goes on to the resurrection. Each station has a foundation in the Scriptures themselves and invites us to reflect on them in this light:

1. Jesus Washes the Feet of His Disciples
   (John 13:2–15)

2. Jesus in the Garden
   (Matt. 26:36–56; Mark 14:32–52; Luke 22:39–53; John 18:1–12)

3. Jesus before the Jewish Authorities
   (Matt. 26:57–75; Mark 14:53–72; Luke 22:54–71; John 18:12–27)

4. Jesus before Pilate
   (Matt. 27:1–26; Mark 15:1–15; Luke 23:1–25;
   John 18:28–19:16)

5. Jesus Is Scourged, Crowned, and Mocked
   (Matt. 27:26–31; Mark 15:15–20)

6. Jesus Takes Up His Cross
   (Mark 15:20; John 17:18)

7. Simon Helps Jesus Carry His Cross
   (Matt. 27:32; Mark 15:21–22; Luke 23:26)

8. Jesus Consoles the Women
   (Luke 23:27–31)

9. Jesus Is Nailed to the Cross
   (Matt. 27:33–38; Mark 15:23–27; Luke 23:33–34;
   John 19:17–24)

10. "This Day You Will Be with Me in Paradise"
    (Luke 23:39–43)

11. "Behold Your Mother"
    (John 19:25–27)

12. Jesus Dies on the Cross
    (Matt. 27:39–56; Mark 15:28–41; Luke 23:44–46;
    John 19:28–37)

13. The Burial of Jesus
    (Matt. 27:57–66; Mark 15:42–47; Luke 23:50–56;
    John 19:38–42)

14. Jesus Rises
    (Matt. 28:1–15; Mark 16:1–13; Luke 24:1–43;
    John 20:1–23)

It would be difficult to formulate many alternative series of Stations of the Cross and still remain within the context of this way of prayer. However, various aspects can be expanded for more extensive consideration (e.g., the fifth station above could be expanded into three stations, the third into two), Peter's denials and each of Jesus' seven last words could be the subject of its own station. The fact that the biblical series has been developed and the pope has felt free to use it indicates a new flexibility in regard to this way of prayer. The sense of moving with Jesus through his passion and especially on the sorrowful way to Calvary should not be lost or we would be moving into an expression of Christian meditation other than the Way of the Cross.

There is in the Way of the Cross a very incarnational symbol. As we enter into this prayer we actually walk with Christ. Our whole body enters into the prayer. It is an incarnate prayer, expressed in our bodies as well as our spirits. Like the fingering of the beads when we pray the rosary, this physical activity helps our attention and devotion. We are conscious of walking with Christ, and that in the most sacred moments of his life. Because the prayer puts us on a path apart from our busy secular life and keeps us there until the fourteen or fifteen stations are trod, it helps us to prolong our prayer with constancy. But this walking also symbolizes what we are doing and what we want as the fruit of the prayer. We are actually walking with Christ in our lives, sharing in his way of suffering that leads to death and life. And our prayer is that our walk, because it is with Christ and is empowered and transformed by his sacred journey to the cross, will in fact lead us and, like Christ's walk and with Christ's walk, lead many others to the victory of resurrection and eternal life. The Stations invite us to be, very consciously for a time, the Christ that we are and to be with the Christ within in the culminating mystery of his passion, death, and resurrection.

When we are to pray the Stations it is well to take a few minutes to prepare. We do not know how to pray as we ought but the Holy Spirit is within, to teach us and to pray with us, to be in a way our prayer. We call upon the Spirit. Then with her help we consciously separate ourselves from our everyday journey and dispose ourselves to walk for a few minutes in another way, the Way of the Cross. We might in imagination transport ourselves to Jerusalem — the Jerusalem of today with its Via Dolorosa or the Jerusalem of twenty centuries ago, walking with Jesus in his own times. Or we might more personally just simply unite ourselves with Jesus or with Mary or another of that time or a later time who has intimately associated himself or herself with this Way and begin to walk with that chosen companion.

Once we are prepared, we walk to the first station. There is a moment of recognition of the event and then we enter into it in the way we have chosen for this particular journey to Calvary. We have spoken above of some of the different possibilities. Depending on the time we have at our disposal, we plan to spend a minute or a few minutes at each station. But always remember, the Stations like the rosary and the Divine Office are a method of prayer. The important thing is

prayer. The whole purpose is prayer. If at the first station or one of the others the Lord moves us to enter
more deeply into prayer, then let the method go and
be with the Lord. There is no necessity to complete
the journey every time we start it. We can always continue the journey the next day. Some people who enjoy
a simpler, more contemplative type of prayer just visit
one station each day and take two weeks to complete
their praying the Way of the Cross.

MOVE WITH GRACE

Ordinarily we will find our meditations on the stations
rather prosaic. Fine. We should spend the allotted time
with the mystery in our chosen way and then move on.
Before moving on if our time has been spent primarily
in discursive reflection, drawing upon the imagination
or reasonings, it might be well to move to a more affective prayer, speaking directly to our Lord or to the
Father. Some like to genuflect or kneel for a moment
when they come to each station and begin with the
traditional salutation:

> We adore you, O Christ, and we praise you
> because by your holy cross you have redeemed the
>   world.

Again, some like to kneel for a bit before leaving
each station for some moments of affective prayer.
Some find it helpful to use the traditional prayer formulas during these moments — the Lord's Prayer, the

angelic salutation, and the doxology — but such formulas, especially when we are praying the Stations alone, are by no means necessary. We are walking with an intimate friend, our Lord and Master, in the most moving moments of his life. Formulas are hardly needed. Be free. Where the Spirit is, there is freedom, says Saint Paul.

Except when you are enjoying a free day, some vacation or retreat time, or are sick in bed, you will probably have to fit the praying of the Stations into a schedule. As I have said, this may establish the expectation of spending a certain amount of time with each station. But move graciously with grace, complete what stations you can, and when the time is up, quietly turn it over to the Lord and ask him to continue to walk with you as you go about your daily journey. If you have not completed the fourteen or fifteen stations, you might want to begin next time where you have left off. If, however, you are finding the first stations most fruitful, do not hesitate to begin with them again. If at a certain time in your life there is one station that, for one reason or another, particularly attracts you, do not hesitate to begin with it each day. Perhaps you will find yourself spending your whole time at that one station. That's fine if it is what is most helping you to enter into a deeper communion with your Lord and Love. Prayer is the thing.

I have just said "each day." Should the Stations be a daily practice? It is a matter of discernment. I have known people who make the stations many times each day. They are privileged in the sense that they have that much time for prayer. At certain periods in our life we will perhaps find the Stations more helpful as a method of prayer than the rosary or the office. So we will give them priority. Time may be a problem for us so that we might just pray the Stations once a week, on Fridays, or on our free days. They may be of more rare occurrence: retreat days, a Lenten practice, or the like. They may prove helpful in times of anguish. Even if we cannot get to church we can hold a crucifix or just fold our hands and mentally walk the Way with Christ. Lying awake on one of those sleepless nights we might find peace (and even sleep) by quietly beginning the Way of the Cross.

The Stations of the Cross, like the awesome reality they make present, are a gift to us, given to us by God through the tradition through the Church. They are ours to use in the way we discern they will best help us to awaken to the reality of our union with Christ in his saving passion. And not just as a historical reality but as actually present, present in and through the NOW of God. The Christ who now walks to Calvary, who suffers and dies as an expression of love for the Father and for us, is right now present within us, one with us, inviting us to be one with him in all, but especially in this supreme act of love.

We walk the Way of the Cross with the Christ within.

CHAPTER FOUR

ANOTHER TRADITION

here is before me on my desk a black cord of knotted beads. In many ways it is apparently not dissimilar from the knotted cord that sits on my night table. In fact, the two cords represent two different Christian traditions.

The one on my night table is actually a rosary, its decades of knots carefully crafted by one of my friends who enjoys the rather unique vocation of being a rosary-maker and spreading devotion to the rosary. The heavy cord he has used has even been woven into a cross at the end of the pendant. It makes a good bed-rosary and has spent many a quiet if sleepless hour with me.

The other cord, the black one on my desk, has sometimes been called a Byzantine rosary. I do not think this is proper. We want to respect all traditions and respect their consecrated terminology. A Christian prayer word is not a mantra, a consecrated term from the Hindu tradition, nor is a prayer cord a rosary. It is a prayer cord.

75

The Greeks call it a *komvoschinion;* the Russians, a *tchotki*. In English they sometimes call it a prayer rope, but more commonly it is called a prayer cord.

My cord is a gift from Father Methodius, a monk of Zographou, one of the twenty ruling monasteries on Mount Athos. It is of the simple monastic type, not one with the color or frills that are sometimes added to prayer cords made for more popular sale. This one has a hundred knots, each of which is made up of some twenty-one knots. (I had watched Father make it while I ate the generous bowl of good thick soup he had set before me when I arrived at his monastery.) As he completed his work, joining the ends of the string of knots to form a circle, he went on to weave a sizeable cross that hangs as a pendant from the chaplet. Some prayer cords have three hundred knots and there are smaller ones of fifty knots. There may be wooden or glass beads inserted among the knotted ones to mark off each twenty-five. These cords are used when praying the Jesus Prayer. Worn on the wrist or carried in the hand they can serve as a reminder, helping one move toward constant prayer.

THE WAY OF THE JESUS PRAYER

The pattern has not changed since the earliest days of the Church. When young Orthodox desire to take their life in Christ more seriously, they will go in search of a spiritual father or mother. They may have to visit many monasteries and churches before they find one to whom they feel they can entrust themselves and who will accept them as a disciple. As disciples they ask, "Father/Mother, give me a word of life." The mentor will then give the disciple a word, usually one drawn from the Sacred Scriptures.

The most common and popular word (word is used here in a broad sense; it may be a single word or a phrase or a sentence) is actually a double word, drawn from the Gospels. You will recall the incident when Jesus was leaving Jericho. There was a blind man sitting by the side of the road, begging. His name was Bartimaeus. When he heard it was Jesus passing by, he cried out in a loud voice: "Lord Jesus, Son of David, have pity on me." When people tried to quiet him, he cried all the louder, until he was finally heard and cured. The second part of the word comes from a story Jesus himself told: Two men went up to the Temple to pray, a Pharisee and a despised tax collector. The Pharisee thought he had it all put together. He thanked God for making him such a grand fellow who did all the right things. On the other hand, the tax collector stood meekly in a back corner, head bowed. As he struck his breast, he prayed, Lord, have mercy on me a sinner. Taking the words of the man who was blind and the public sinner, the Fathers fashioned this word: "Lord Jesus Christ, Son of the living God, have mercy on me a sinner." They held that this short word did in fact contain the whole of the revelation.

The disciple is given a word. He is then told to do perhaps ten *komvoschinion* and fifty prostrations. This means that he is to stand before the icon, looking into the face of Christ — our Byzantine brothers and sisters find a real presence in the icon — with prayer cord in hand. As each knot passes through his fingers, the disciple repeats the word he has received. When he has gone round the cord ten times, has recited his word five hundred times, he will begin his prostrations, again reciting his word as he falls to the floor. The prostration might be the little *metonia* or the great. For the little *metonia* he goes down on his knees, touches his knuckles to the ground and bows deeply. For the great *metonia*, he prostrates full length.

The repetition, especially the repetition with prostrations, is to allow the word to sink deeper and deeper into the disciple, forming his or her heart. The classical way the Fathers express this is "to bring the mind down into the heart."

When evening comes the disciple goes to see his spiritual father. He would then "manifest his thoughts." He will share with the father the thoughts that came to his consciousness as he recited the word and made his prostrations. On the basis of this manifestation the father judges the disciple's progress and, as appropriate, modifies the "obedience." He might increase or diminish the number of *komvoschinion* or the number of prostrations. Or he might modify the word itself. If the manifestation indicated that the disciple was very conscious of his sinfulness and much in need of purification and enlightenment, the father might tell him simply to say: Lord, Jesus, be merciful to me a sinner. If the disciple is moving more fully toward enlightenment, she might be told to pray: Lord

Jesus Christ, Son of God — her prayer becoming more simply one of adoration. Eventually the prayer comes to be one simple word: Jesus. That is enough. The prostrations come to rest in one prolonged one. Or perhaps the disciple will simply stand before the icon or sit in a quiet, composed manner, achieving an ever greater stability of mind, body, and spirit. The word becomes rarer as the mind stills more and more. He has found the holy rest of contemplation.

No direct effort is made to achieve this state. To strive for the state itself would be to turn what is supposed to be prayer into some sort of technique to attain something for one's self. The prayer would have become a project of the false self. Stillness is a by-product. As the presence of God fills the mind and heart more and more, purifying it and driving out all else, peace, order, tranquility, silence come to reign. The disciple has less and less to manifest to the father.

Ordinarily speaking, this process moves along most expeditiously if the disciple can abide with the spiritual father or is able to come to him each evening for the manifestation. When this is not possible, then the fine honing of the prayer moves along less sensitively. The disciple comes to the father when he can and the father gives what direction the manifestation calls for.

But remember we are not speaking about something that is "ordinary." All of this is in the realm of grace, or should be. We do not know how to pray as we ought, even with the best of fathers or mothers guiding us. It is the work of the Spirit, who prays within us. If one is open and disposed and does what he can by way of getting guidance and practicing the prayer, the Spirit will not fail such a faithful one.

The lament is often heard, even in Orthodox circles and much more in the West and among Westerners, that it is difficult to find a spiritual father or mother. The Hindus have a saying: When the disciple is ready, the guru will appear. I think this has some real validity. One of the best spiritual fathers I know has said to me: the problem is not a lack of spiritual fathers; it is lack of those who *really* want a spiritual father. Few are ready to be faithful to a rigorous practice that will be enforced by the accountability of daily or regular meetings with a loved and loving father, whose love does not hold back from a certain due severity. Among those who are willing to go this far there will not be many who are ready to go further into a complete and honest manifestation of thoughts. Just take a moment and think of all the ridiculous, sublime, sordid, and queer thoughts that have flashed across your mind. How ready are you to share all of these with another human being? Add to these the thoughts that would inevitably arise in regard to the father himself. To want to lay it all out there takes a humility and courage that can come only from grace and an ardent desire inflamed by a deep insight into how precious is purity of heart and how it is indeed worth such a price.

This is, indeed, the goal of this practice, a purity of heart that enables one to be simply before the eyes of God, totally revealed, so pure, so clear, that no thought mars the surface. The undistorted image, reflecting him of whom it is the image and absorbing all the love that comes forth from the Source. A total and perfect communion of love. Words fail to express this adequately, but something deep within us resonates and tells us that this is the kind of communion our being cries out for.

But what if, in truth, we cannot find a father or mother who will work with us in this process of deification. What then are we to do? I once addressed this question to a spiritual father in a little Orthodox monastery that was a bit of Mount Athos translated to the new world. His answer was quite simple: If you cannot find a father, you have the Fathers. Go to the Fathers of the Church. They live now in the Lord. They can speak to you and guide you through their writings. I believe this father was speaking from a lived experience. When he spoke of Saint John Chrysostom he spoke in such a way that I received the distinct impression that he and Saint John had had frequent intimate discourse.

At first sight, though, this would not seem to be an adequate response. The writings of the Fathers are rather general teaching. If they should, in a particular case, be addressed to a particular disciple, then they are particular to that disciple. How do they respond to the very personal direction we need in pursuing this way of prayer? There is something of mystery here. The words are but the vehicle of a more personal communication. The Father, alive in God, can be immediately present to us in his writings. The Spirit who inspired him as he wrote the words is also present, present in us as Teacher. She can use the words to speak to us now or to let the Father speak to us. These are communica-

tions at the level of grace, faith, and the gifts of the
Holy Spirit. Judging from the fruit in the lives of some
who speak from experience, they are a reality and op-
erate as a sure guide when the Lord decides to work in
one's life this way.

Perhaps, though, a more real question for most of us
is this: what if we would like to follow this way of prayer
but we really are not ready to go all the way with it? Can
the way of the Jesus Prayer be used by those who want
a deeper prayer life, a deeper union with the Lord, but
are not ready to dedicate themselves to such a wholehearted pursuit of purity of heart as the full practice of
this way calls for?

Let me respond to this in this way. I believe every
legitimate way of prayer, if it is pursued with fidelity,
will in time lead us to complete purity of heart and
union with God, to a deep contemplative union with
God. I have seen the rosary do this and certainly Centering Prayer. Active ways of prayer, like the Stations,
almost begin to demand that we lay aside their activity
and enter into a more contemplative expression that is
their natural consummation. I do not believe the Jesus
Prayer is that different from other ways of prayer. If we
begin this way of prayer as best we can, quietly reciting
the prayer with recollection, give a determined period
of time each day over to this practice, and are faithful
to it, the prayer itself will lead and call us forth. The
use of an icon or turning to the true icon within helps
the recollection. Prostrations help incarnate the prayer.
These are usually more helpful at the beginning, getting us beyond some of our sloth as we devote more

of our energies to the practice of prayer. If we add to this the practice of taking some time after our prayer to examine the thoughts that spontaneously came up during the prayer, this will, if we use this insight properly and do not turn it into a self-preoccupation, help us to move toward an increasing self-knowledge. This in turn should challenge us to seek a greater generosity of spirit and purity of heart. The practice, thus pursued, especially if it is within the context of a more common and general spiritual guidance, should be a fruitful one for the average serious Christian person who is attracted to it.

What makes the full practice of the way of the Jesus Prayer such a demanding practice and so directly effective in achieving purity of heart is its combination with the manifestation of thoughts to a skilled spiritual father or mother. If I can be excused for what might seem like a rather gross analogy in what is a most sensitive and sublime matter, I could liken this to working with a skilled coach. An average, sensible adult who wants to keep in reasonably good health will undertake a regular exercise program. He will probably choose an exercise he likes and will therefore find it less difficult to remain faithful. He will give regular time to it and perform it in a way that is perhaps quite creditable. He will achieve his end, the maintenance of a good physical condition. But he will never be a gold medalist in the sport he is engaging in. One who really wants to become proficient in a particular sport will seek out a good coach and place himself under his supervision. He will faithfully carry out the regime that the coach outlines for him: run so many miles, do so many pushups, and so forth. And he will perform in the presence of the coach, letting the coach see exactly what he is doing so that the coach can constantly fine-tune his coaching.

The analogy limps, of course. One does not undertake a prayer practice just to keep in good spiritual health. Relationships do not work that way. They either grow or deteriorate. As a relationship grows it necessarily becomes more demanding even while it becomes more satisfying and even delightful. If we decide not to meet the arising demands of the deepening relationship — not to move toward proficiency (to return to the analogy) — the relationship immediately begins to deteriorate. To use another more traditional analogy, one does not stand still on the ladder to heaven. One goes up or one goes down.

But we do have to face the fact that our going up sometimes is half-hearted. We do not put our whole heart into our progress. We are not open to a vigorous coaching. I hope this does not place us in the category of the lukewarm whom our Lord feels like vomiting out of his mouth. But we all do struggle with faintheartedness. We can all profit by a coach. We do need at least a partner to jog at our side and help us keep going.

If we are really honest we realize that there are choices to be made here and consequences to be paid. If we do place ourselves in the hands of a good spiritual father or mother, it will not be easy, but we will reap a progress that bears the fruits of the Spirit: love, joy, peace, patience, kindness. If we do not seek such spiritual coaching our progress will not be as steady, the fruit of our spiritual disciplines and practices will not be so abundant, we will have to contend more with the outcroppings of the capital sins: pride, covetousness, lust, anger, gluttony, envy, and sloth. The choice is ours. And it is a choice we often prefer to duck. But ducking it is only another way of saying no. And we reap the consequences of a no. We cannot really escape it, even if we kid ourselves into thinking we do.

In this volume we speak of various spiritual practices. All of them will be more effectively present in our lives if we practice them with great openness under the guidance of a devoted spiritual father or mother. Accountability greatly facilitates fidelity and the clarity of openness creates wonderful space for the practice to be effective in our lives.

Yes, the Jesus Prayer can be practiced without our necessarily engaging in the full rigors of "manifestation of thoughts." But if we are fortunate enough to have someone who is willing to accompany us in this way on the spiritual journey, we would be very foolish not to avail ourselves of this great grace.

Have we said all there is to be said about the practice of the Jesus Prayer? What about the practices set forth in *The Way of the Pilgrim* and the oddities depicted in *Franny and Zooey* — if perhaps you have read that novel?

Historically, as we have seen, the Jesus Prayer comes from the earliest Christian experience. It has the same origin as the Centering Prayer. Seekers went to spiritual fathers and mothers, received an evangelical word of life, and, through a carefully guided practice, interiorized the word until it formed the heart and called forth a response. We can see that this is but another expression of the basic way of *lectio divina*. The word of revelation in this case is received from the spiritual father or mother. The careful repetition of it with the rope and prostrations, a repetition that easily flows over into the rest of the practitioner's life, is precisely *meditatio*, leading to the response of *oratio*. The guided simplification leads to a very pure *contemplatio*. The final practice of the Jesus Prayer is exactly the same as Centering Prayer (about which we will speak in the next chapter) except that in the case of the Jesus Prayer, the prayer word in the end is always "Jesus."

This is the way the Jesus Prayer was practiced in the earliest centuries. This is the way it is practiced today in Russia and Maldavia and on the Holy Mountain. However, in the intervening centuries, Byzantine Christianity fell under a long-perduring domination by Islam. It was inevitable that the dominant social culture, which was in its own way a religious culture, would influence the culture, life, and practices of the people it dominated. Thus in the later Middle Ages we find spiritual masters of the Orthodox tradition, such as Gregory of Sinai, Andrew of Crete, Nesophorus of Jerusalem, and above all Gregory Palamas, introducing into the practice of the Jesus Prayer certain psychosomatic elements that were prevalent in the practice of the devout Muslim Sufis. More emphasis was placed on posture. Kneeling down in a crouching position, pressing the chin into the chest, was to help bring the mind down into the heart. Various rhythms in the breathing were tied to the repetition of the prayer, facilitating its constant repetition. Imaging was employed. And enormous numbers of repetitions were assigned to the disciple.

It is obvious that unless a certain amount of careful guidance is present and a good bit of discretion these practices can bring about stress and strain and even lead to mental unbalance, as unfortunately they often enough have. This is what Salinger was pointing to in *Franny and Zooey. The Way of the Pilgrim* is somewhat mythological in its presentation of the practice of the Jesus Prayer. An unguided attempt to follow literally the way as it is depicted there is bound to lead to tragedy. It certainly will not lead to the sanctity envisioned by the early Fathers who gently if strictly guided their disciples.

Theophane the Recluse, one of the great Russian spiritual fathers of the last century, led the way to reform and renewal in the practice of the Jesus Prayer. He urged that all the psychosomatic practices that had come in from other traditions should be laid aside and that masters and disciples should return to the simple, pure method of the early Fathers and Mothers. His words have prevailed in many corners, the corners in which the prayer is most sincerely practiced today.

Some good guidance is available for those who want to understand this way more fully and perhaps even enter into the practice of it. The whole of the *Philokalia* has been translated and published in English by Bishop Kallistos Ware with the help of others. Bishop Ware himself has published an excellent booklet on the Jesus

Prayer. Father Irenee Hausherr's *The Name of Jesus*, also available in English thanks to Cistercian Publications, gives us a full and rich understanding of this tradition.

A word that is useful in regard to all prayer and every form of prayer applies, perhaps preeminently here: Keep it simple — especially if you are entering into this practice without the personal guidance of a true master. Sometimes when people speak of the Jesus Prayer they mean simply to use the favored word, "Lord Jesus Christ, Son of the living God, have mercy on me a sinner," and to recite it frequently as a sort of ejaculatory prayer. There is no danger in this. As certainly there is no danger in using the Jesus Prayer in its most ancient and simple way, a way very similar to that of Centering Prayer. Our caution surrounds the use of psychosomatic techniques that may not be fully understood or applied with enough delicacy and insight. A practice that seeks altered physiological and psychological states or various experiences is in great danger of being a project of the false self rather than a pure prayer that truly seeks God and God alone.

I do not want to end on a negative note. I would not have devoted a chapter to the consideration of the Jesus Prayer if I did not think of it as a way that has something to offer us. Its long and varied history teaches us in many ways. The saints who have practiced it truly edify. The wonderful stories in the *Philokalia* can enlighten and encourage anyone's spiritual practice. Some persons are called to walk in the way of the Jesus Prayer. Blessed are they, especially if they have a true spiritual mother or father to guide them. I have met such fathers and mothers in my journeys, even in America, and I have felt myself blessed in being able to speak with them for a few passing hours. Their disciples are truly blessed.

To those, however, who will not be able to enjoy the careful and caring guidance of such a mentor I would suggest you read on. I believe the simple traditional teaching of the Centering Prayer, which comes from the same source, can safely guide one in the development of the practice of the Jesus Prayer in its more advanced and contemplative stages. I have on more than one occasion been honored by our Orthodox brethren by being asked to speak to them in precisely this regard. They have found the teaching very practical and very helpful even as they pursued their own proper tradition and lived ever in the beautiful and transforming way of the Jesus Prayer.

CHAPTER FIVE

TRANSFORMATIVE BEING

We have talked about *lectio*, listening, receiving the Word of God, and *meditatio*, allowing the Word of God to rest within us and form our hearts, which blossoms forth in *oratio*, true prayer, communication, communion, and union with God, leading to *contemplatio*, a simple, wholehearted being with God.

We can see how the rosary is a *lectio*. We might even take up the Sacred Scriptures and read the related passages as we begin each decade. The so-called Scriptural Rosary would have us read a sentence of Scripture before each bead. Then as we enter into the Aves we enter into a *meditatio*. We let the event as it has been revealed to us, through what we have just read or heard from the leader or as it resides in our memories, be present to us, forming our hearts and calling forth a re-

91

sponse, *oratio*. We have seen that this may become a simple *contemplatio*, as we simply hold the rosary in hand or almost unconsciously recite the prayers while we rest deeply in the Lord.

The Stations, too, are an expression of this basic prayer pattern. We could actually bring our Bible with us and read the relevant passages as we move along the Way of the Cross, especially if we are using the Biblical Stations. More often we will probably call forth from our memories what has been revealed to us in previous readings or other experiences. We move readily into meditation. The more ancient tradition of *meditatio* invites us to approach the Stations in what might be a deeper and more formative way. Instead of contenting ourselves with thoughts and images, working over the matter with our human reason, albeit informed by faith, we might just let the fullness of the reality of each stational event impress itself upon our hearts. Like Mary (and with Mary, if we will) we can ponder the event in our heart — let it be there forming our heart and calling us forth to an integral and even transcendent experience of it. *Oratio* flows spontaneously out of this *meditatio*. If we are employing a more rational or imaginative type of meditation we have to take care that we do not get so caught up in our own thoughts and images that we never move on to prayer, to actually communicating with the Lord as present with us. *Meditatio* will also move us on spontaneously to *contemplatio*. With the Stations, though, when grace moves us in this direction, we will have to be ready to leave off our journeying on the Way for the moment and settle where we are: Be still and know that I am God. Contemplation calls us to simply be to God, letting everything else go. When our total attention is given to one we can hardly attend to another. The wonder of it is that when we do attend to this One we do in some way actually find all in our God. But that is the secret of the contemplative. (And by contemplative I do not mean just one who is canonically living in the contemplative state of life; I mean anyone who gives himself or herself to contemplative prayer — let that be clear. All are invited by the Lord to enjoy the holy rest of contemplation.)

We have seen, too, how the way of the Jesus Prayer is ordered to leading the one who practices it faithfully to move from *lectio* to *meditatio* and *oratio* and on to contemplative rest.

CONTEMPLATION

So let us now turn our attention to this contemplative rest, to contemplation. But first a word of warning. Contemplation must not be seen as a goal, as something to be achieved by us, a state to be attained. God alone is the goal. Union and communion with God is what we want, what we are made for, what God made us for. If we start concentrating on the union, the communion, the contemplation, this itself prevents us from attaining what we seek. Our intent must be wholly on God and this will bring about the union and communion and the deep, renewing contemplative rest.

A purity of heart is needed here. This is why spiritual teachers and writers have made so much of asceticism. They saw clearly this need of purity of heart. But again there is a danger here. Asceticism can become the project. Attaining purity of heart can become the project. And we are again back to ourselves, seeking something for ourselves, albeit in theory it is for God and to prepare us for union with God.

The matter is so subtle. The false self is very sly. It will insinuate itself into anything we undertake. We have to be as wise as serpents and as simple as doves. The simpler, the more clear and direct we are in our pursuit of God, the better chance we will have of avoiding the wiles of the false self that so often undermine the best efforts of the best of us. The simple ancient method of prayer that has come to be called in our time Centering Prayer is a most effective help here, if it is practiced with a certain tenacious persistence.

CENTERING PRAYER

Let me describe this way of prayer. I will be rather brief here for I have written a number of books on it, and Father Thomas Keating has also written on it with masterly insight.

Centering Prayer is a new name for a very ancient form of prayer. Its origins are the same as that of the Jesus Prayer, only in this case it was a Westerner, John

Cassian by name, who went in search of a spiritual father. He found one in Abba Isaac, who was reputed to be the holiest and oldest and wisest father among the fathers in the Egyptian desert at that time, the end of the fourth century. John's quest had been a long one and he was filled with joy when the holy old man taught him how to find contemplative peace. Later John himself became a spiritual father and a community of men as well as a community of women gathered around him after he returned to the West. For these disciples he undertook to write down what he had learned from the venerated father in the desert.

A century later another great spiritual father rose up in the West. His name was Benedict, from Nursia. He wrote his Rule for Monasteries, which became very popular. In this rule he recommended that his disciples turn to John Cassian and John's record of the conferences of Abba Isaac and others for deeper, richer spiritual teaching. Thus the teaching John received in the desert passed into the mainstream of Western spirituality.

We find it developed in the earliest spiritual writings we have in English. One in particular, that of a father who humbly hid in anonymity, became very popular and has held its popularity through all the following centuries. This little work, called *The Cloud of Unknowing*, written for one of the father's spiritual sons, is not easy to read because it belongs to a time long past, but the essence of the teaching is there with much wise counsel. This treatise and many others give witness to how widely this sort of contemplative prayer was practiced among the people. It was not the preserve of monks and nuns though they were the principal teachers. Because they were the teachers, when the monasteries were destroyed during the Protestant Reformation and the French Revolution, the practice of this form of prayer was largely lost. It is only in our times that it is again being widely taught and practiced among the faithful.

Traditionally this way of prayer has had many names. It is the culmination of *lectio* and so did not need a particular name. It is *contemplatio*. It is prayer in the heart; the mind, the attention, comes down into the heart and abide quietly there. To achieve this Abba Isaac counseled Cassian to be content with the poverty of a single simple word. The author of *The Cloud of Unknowing* pressed this further: Choose a simple word, a single-syllable word is best, like "God" or "love." Choose a word that is meaningful to you, the meaning being: I am all yours, Lord. This little word is fixed in the mind. It represents God and only God. It abides there, keeping the mind and heart in God. Anything else that comes along is simply let go. This little word is our sole response, God is our sole care during this time of love. It is simple as that.

The word has its power and meaning for it is the fruit of *lectio*. *Contemplatio* always presupposes *lectio*. All prayer is a response. God speaks to us. We allow his word to come alive in us. It forms us and calls us into ever deeper union. It transforms us until we have the mind and heart of Christ.

To facilitate the teaching and practice of this very

traditional prayer form we have set it forth in three simple points, with a bit of a preface and a final word. Let us look at these now.

The preface concerns posture at prayer. Some traditions make more of this than others. This tradition keeps it simple. Sit quietly: that is all the author of *The Cloud of Unknowing* has to say about posture. Sit quietly. That means finding a place where we can expect to be left undisturbed while praying. This may mean putting a note on our door. Though it is quite possible to sit in a library or an airport (not to speak of a church) or some other public place and feel confident that no one will bother us. A quiet place is perhaps more helpful, especially when we are first beginning the prayer and have not developed the facility to let sounds go by. Sit quietly. Find a good chair. Let the body be settled comfortably. Not too comfortably — or we will soon be snoring. If our back is well supported and relatively straight the energies can freely flow up and down the spinal system, a part of the refreshment and renewal the prayer affords. We close the eyes gently, fostering the inner quiet, the movement to that place within, the center, where God, the source of our being, dwells.

So, sit quietly, the back straight and well supported, the eyes gently closed, in a place where you can expect to be left undisturbed.

Enough for the preface; let us look at the Centering Prayer method itself:

1. *Be in faith and love to God who dwells within.*

"Be" — Centering is a prayer of being, not of thinking, saying, imagining, feeling, or doing anything but

simply being to God, with God in love. We do not give
God our thoughts or words or images or feelings. We
give God our very selves. We simply "are" to God.

"In faith" — Faith is the wonderful gift from God by
which we *know* that whatever God has said is true, because God can never deceive nor be deceived. And God
has told us that he will dwell within us. "The Father
and I will come and we will make our dwelling within
you."

"And love" — Love is gift. I remember a line from a
song: Love is not love until it is given away. Love is a
giveaway. We simply give ourselves to God. For these
twenty minutes we are all his for God to do with us
whatever God wishes. We are willing to let all our own
thoughts, ideas, plans, aspirations, and doings go and
simply rest with God and let God do whatever he wants
with us during this time of love.

"To God ... within" — God is everywhere. It is possible to center upon God in others and in other things.
Catholics have often enough been naturally led to
center upon our Lord present in the tabernacle. Our
Orthodox brothers and sisters often center on God
present within the icon. We might choose to center
upon the Lord present in the heart of Mary. We can
center upon the Lord in a the living flame of a can-
dle or in the beauty of a flower or even in a sound,
but there is danger here of getting centered in the out-
ward sign and not in the imageless God within. God is
everywhere, but his chosen dwelling, the place where
he abides in love with the one whom he loves, is deep
within, at the center and ground of our being. Of all the

icons this is the best, for we are each the icon God has made of himself, the true icon made in his own image and likeness. God is within. In the Centering Prayer we very simply rest within with him.

This in essence is the whole of the prayer: simply resting with God in love. In order to facilitate our resting there with him we have a second point.

2. *Take up a love word and let it be gently present, supporting your being to God in faith-filled love.*

"*A love word*" or a prayer word — As we have seen, the Fathers recommend a very simple word, even going so far as to say it should be a single-syllable word. But always remember: Where the Spirit is, there is freedom. Choose what is for you a meaningful word, the meaning being: I am all yours, God. We do not need to repeat this word constantly as one might repeat a mantra. The word is there, a little arrow, pointing us wholly to the Lord, our love. We let it, as it were, gently repeat itself if it will. We rest in God.

Alas, soon enough, if the Lord does not embrace us with a most special love — and he sometimes does — we will discover ourselves off chasing some thought or memory or feeling or plan or fear or. . . .

And so we need a third point.

3. *Whenever, during the time of your prayer, you become aware of anything, simply, gently return to the Lord, with the use of your word.*

"*During the time of your prayer*" — We usually recommend twenty minutes twice a day. Morning and evening prayer at the cardinal points of the day seems to be universally recommended. What we do know is that those who center twice a day much more quickly arrive at a centered life, a life filled with the fruits of centering: love, joy, peace, patience, kindness, gentleness, benignity.... The experience of many — and I mean many, thousands upon thousands — recommends twenty minutes. Yet again, where the Spirit is, there is freedom. Experience will lead some individuals to choose a longer or shorter period. And many will choose to have more than two periods a day. In any case, during the time of our prayer we are willing to let God take care of his creation. It is the time for love. We have twenty-three plus hours to attend to others and their needs and to attend to God himself in the many other wonderful ways in which we can pray and listen to him. For now, it is the time to rest in love. This time, which the Beloved loves, will give depth and richness to all the other times and all the doings of life. So...

"Whenever... we become aware of anything" — Good, bad or indifferent, no matter what our mind or imagination, our hearing or our feelings serve up, our response is ever the same. During this time, as soon as we become aware, as soon as our attention is no longer 100 percent on God, we gently turn back to God himself with the use of our little word of love. We want to love him with our whole mind, our whole heart, our whole soul, and all our strength.

"Simply, gently" — No big show about it. Otherwise the fuss itself might take us more away from God than the grabbing thought or image. Simply: back to God. We do not try to get rid of the thoughts or images. We

will never succeed in this. We simply turn to God, and as we turn to him we automatically turn away from them. We are gentle with ourselves, knowing that we will ever be having thoughts and images and desires and feelings. There is nothing wrong in this. The moment of awareness is the moment of choice. I choose God — gently, using my love word — and again I am centered. Each time I return to the Lord, I choose him again; it is a perfect act of love. He so gently asks us: Do you love me more than these? And we answer so gently with our word: Yes.

This is the little method passed down through the centuries. Although I have been centering for over forty years and have shared with thousands who have been enjoying the fruits of Centering Prayer in their lives, I am yet amazed how such a simple little thing as sitting quietly with the Lord for twenty minutes twice a day can have such a transforming effect. Yet it does.

And the "final word": At the end of the twenty minutes, let the prayer word go and let the Lord's Prayer (or some other favorite prayer) quietly pray itself within.

We leave the quiet rest of contemplation and enter into a more active prayer as we prepare to return to our active lives. Jesus gave us something wonderful in the Lord's Prayer. It is not just a prayer formula, it is a whole school of prayer, a school of life. If we let it gently, unhurriedly unfold within us it will teach us many things, teach us more and more deeply. During these minutes of quiet emergence, some of the deep things the Lord was teaching us in the silence will now come to the surface of our minds to be carried back into life's activity. These two or three minutes can be very rich. So we do not want to hurry them.

Here then is the simple traditional way of entering into contemplative prayer that comes to us through the centuries and is now set forth in a simple, practical "packaging":

CENTERING PRAYER

Sit quietly, eyes gently closed.

1. *Be in faith and love to God who dwells within.*

2. *Take up a love word and let it be gently present, supporting your being to God in faith-filled love.*

3. *Whenever, during the time of your prayer, you become aware of anything, simply, gently return to the Lord, with the use of your word.*

At the end of the twenty minutes, let the prayer word go and let the Lord's Prayer (or some other favorite prayer) quietly pray itself within.

THE FRUITS OF CENTERING PRAYER

I hesitate to speak about the fruits of contemplation. Contemplation is in a way a sheer waste. It is Mary breaking open the costly alabaster jar of fragrant perfume and letting the whole of its costly content gush out on the feet of the Lord. Contemplation is a luxury that the Christian can ill afford. There is so much to be done. Our option for the poor cries out to us to make better use of our scant time. Yet it is a luxury we can ill afford to do without. Because our Lord wants it, wants it very much. And because if we do not heed his call — Come to me all you who labor and are heavily burdened and I will refresh you — we will not long be able to do anything else of true worth and effectiveness.

Yet if we begin to detail the rich fruits that flow from this little practice of love, there is much danger that we will vitiate the offering; we will begin to seek the fruits and turn our prayer into a project of the false self instead of a gift of purest love. If, in fact, we do this, we will frustrate ourselves. For when we begin to seek something for ourselves rather than giving ourselves in purest love to the Lord, we no longer truly center and the fruits will no longer be produced.

The false self is made up of what I do, what I have, and what others think of me. (That last one has a real hook in us: what others think of me!) This is the self that Jesus said must die — so that our true self can emerge. When we center we really "kill" the false self. For what are we doing? Just sitting there, wasting time in love. Nothing for which to pat ourselves on the back. And who else will think much of us for just sitting there: Lord, tell her to get up and help. And what do we have. Nothing (but God himself!). We let go of all our doings and thinkings and plannings, even our thoughts. Our thoughts are the last bastion of the false self. Take away everything else from me, at least I know what I think. But in Centering Prayer we give up even our thoughts. This goes right to the heart of the false self. The prevailing philosophy of our times claims: *Cogito, ergo sum*. I think, therefore I am. (This is really just the opposite of reality: I am [a human person by God's wondrous mercy and creation] and therefore I think.) The false self tries to create ourselves with our own thoughts. But in centering we give up on this project. We let go of the false self; we die to the false self to live to God.

And what freedom we find. We no longer have to worry about what others think. We know how precious we are in the eyes of God. If others do not appreciate us, they are really missing something. We are free. We can do all things in him who strengthens us. We can have all we want, for he has said, Ask and you shall receive. All is ours and we are Christ's and Christ is God's. Alleluia!

No wonder we are filled with joy and peace and want truly to love everyone and care for everyone.

Natively speaking, we have a certain listening, a certain way in which we allow life and all that is speak to us. It is a listening that is formed by a thousand antecedents. If we are a very prejudiced person, the parameters of our listening are very fixed. Only what fits within them is really heard by us and that is little enough. If we are striving to be more open, then other people and new experiences can come along and stretch our parameters and we can hear more, little by little. But there is still so much that cannot fit within. And God — how little of his immense goodness and love we perceive. But when we come to Centering Prayer, we drop all our parameters. We do not try to fit God or anyone or anything into our ideas or concepts or images.

We let all of these go. We sit there, open and vulnerable, and allow the Divine to invade us and stretch us, or better, totally draw us out into the immensity of his own being.

There is nothing outside now. It is all within. We find everyone within the same Divine Center. We are all one. This is why Centering Prayer so empowers ministry. We come to each and every one as our very self: Love your neighbor *as yourself.* (Not "as if he were yourself," but as yourself: he is yourself in the oneness we are in Christ.) We know we are one in God. My neighbor is myself. How can I not want for her all that I want for myself. It is impossible not to. We are one.

Centering Prayer is a deeply healing prayer. As I rest there deeply in the Lord, the free flow of thoughts and memories, of which I have virtually no awareness, for my attention is wholly set on the Lord even though my rational mind is still functioning, is washing away the hurts and pains, the scars and wounds, the psychological bindings of the past, the past deeply buried in my psyche and now allowed to flow freely up and out. "Come to me you who are heavily burdened and I will refresh you." Jesus is still the physician who comes to heal those who have need. In centering we lay ourselves completely open to his healing ministry, not placing any of our limitations on what he can do. Our psychological defenses are all down. We are wide open. And little by little, as we faithfully center day after day, the healing goes on till we find in our lives a new freedom to love ourselves and everyone else, for now we see ourselves as one with everyone else, the beautiful one reflected in the eyes of the Beloved.

This is the inner reality of the mystery of Church; this is the ultimate meaning of Eucharist. It is really only those who have come to this contemplative insight who can truly understand what it is to pray as Church, what it is to enter into Eucharist. Let us look at these realities that are meant not only to foster the contemplative dimension of life but to be its adequate expression.

CHAPTER SIX

HOURS THAT SANCTIFY THE DAY

I am sure you recall that delightful story in the Acts of the Apostles. Peter and John are going up to the Temple to pray. It is time for the ninth hour, about three in the afternoon. As they approach the Golden Gate a crippled man, sitting on the ground near the entry, makes his pitiful plea. The two apostles stop. The man looks expectantly. Most pass him by without a glance. Even those who throw a coin usually do so without stopping. But these two, with such kindly faces, rough like those of men who have worked out in the elements but with dancing eyes — they have actually stopped and are looking, smiling at him. Then he hears those bewildering words: No gold. No silver. But what we have is yours, brother. In the Name, walk! A firm hand grasps his, a firmer faith tugs at his. His rubbery legs hold. No, don't walk — *dance!* And leap for joy.

This delightful incident in the acts or doings of the apostles has many things to tell us. I want to note a couple here in connection with the topic we are entering upon. Acts tell us that Peter and John were going up to the Temple at the time of prayer, the ninth hour. We see then that the apostles, the first Christians, continued to observe the Jewish hours of prayer. This observance, which sanctified the hours of the night and the day, was one of the many things that continued to have life and give life in the new dispensation.

We also note that though Peter and John were on their way to prayer, they did not think this excused them from attending to their brother in his need. The Liturgy of the Hours, or the Divine Office as it is often called, may be a bounden duty for some of us. Others feel strongly called to it by a movement of interior grace. Prayer is important. But we cannot use prayer, even the Divine Office, the prayer of the Church, as an excuse for passing Christ by in his little and needy ones when he is calling to us in them. That is where, at such a moment, he wants our prayerful response. Peter and John stopped. They remembered Jesus' words: Whatever you do to my least one, you do to me. They first prayed to Jesus in speaking to him in the cripple before they went into the Temple to speak to him in the house of his Father.

The Liturgy of the Hours is a very beautiful and a very special prayer. It is in a special way the prayer of the Church, of the whole Body in and through its Head.

It is a powerful means of sanctifying the hours of the day and night. It is a great help in our effort to fulfill the divine command to pray without ceasing. And it helps us to take more and more conscious possession of the reality that we are members of the living body of the Church, called to make our contribution to the vitality of that body even while we are nurtured and supported by it.

Like every other means, every other practice of the Christian life, we must not let it as a means get in the way of the end. We pray to be in ever deeper communion with our Lord. God is where his will is. If the Lord wants us to be outside attending to a beggar, we will never find him inside, even if we are singing psalms with the saints and angels. Our practice of the Liturgy of the Hours needs, then, to fit realistically into the pattern of our lives according to our particular vocation. The full practice of the Liturgy of the Hours, to which monks and nuns are called and which they are given the freedom to undertake, can inspire each and every Christian to find our own way to sanctify the hours through a practice of prayer.

WATCHING IN THE NIGHT

For nuns and monks one of the most important and by far the fullest of the prayer hours is the one spent watching in the night—vigils, or matins as it is sometimes called. This watch is inspired not only by the services in the night in the Temple at Jerusalem, but more intimately by the practice of our Lord. Night after night, even during the busy years of his public ministry, Jesus slipped off to spend some hours communing with his Father. It is in union with Christ that we Christians watch in the night. Like him we find strength here, enlightenment and guidance. Here we praise and thank the Father for his constant presence and love. Here we rest in the Lord and let him take pleasure in us his beloved children.

There is another aspect to watching in the night. If we watch with Christ, we also watch for Christ, for his coming in the dawn, the day that shall come upon us from on high to give light to those who sit in darkness and in the shadow of death, to guide our feet into the way of peace. We wait for the coming of the risen Lord, which enables us to break forth from the tomb of our sin to share in his new and risen life. We wait for his second coming, when he shall lead us all forth into the kingdom of the Father.

The night is indeed a time for watching.

Through hymns that bring us into the particular mystery of the day or season, through psalms that lead us deeply into the paradoxes of salvation history, and through readings that encourage and inspire us by the previous works of the Lord and the example of his holy ones, our minds are enlightened and our wills made strong to pursue more resolutely our own call in this ever-unfolding mystery of salvation.

Saint Benedict of Nursia wrote his Rule for Monasteries in the year 525. Because of its moderation and balance it gradually came to prevail as *the* rule for monks and nuns in the West. The wise legislator provided that his monks should rise only at the seventh hour of the night, about 2:00 A.M., after they had been adequately rested and had been able to digest their food. Thus with wakeful minds and unburdened bodies they could watch and listen and be enlightened and encouraged.

Modern society does not make it easy for us to rise in the night. Few go to bed with the sun. Many activities call upon our evening hours. In recognition of this, in the renewal of the Liturgy of the Hours, the Church has proposed a new outlook on this office. It is not now proposed as a watching in the night but is seen rather as an Office of Readings. The same elements are there: hymn, psalms, readings, and prayer. And they have much the same purposes: to bring us into the particular mystery of the day or season, to lead us deeply into the paradoxes of salvation history, and to encourage and inspire us so that with enlightened minds and wills made strong we can more resolutely pursue our own call in the ever-unfolding mystery of salvation.

This Office of Readings can find its place in our day wherever it is most convenient and suitable for us. It can be the context of our daily *lectio*, the readings offered by the Church being the vehicle through which the Lord speaks to us. It is meant to be a restful, refreshing time. The aspect of watching should not be wholly absent. The Christian is ever watchful, awaiting the coming of the Lord. We hope each day as we enter into the Office of Readings that the Lord will indeed come and speak to us. We pray with hope and expectation and then listen with openness and longing.

The full Office of Readings as found in the Book of Hours, or breviary, as it is sometimes called, may not readily fit into the lives of many. As it is set forth it is meant to nourish the lives especially of priests, who by their ordination have been constituted mediators. Prayer is a supreme element in their lives. Like Peter and the others first ordained, they have to let deacons and others tend to many of the affairs of the life of the Church so that they can give themselves to a ministry of prayer and mediation and of that effective preaching that comes from a deep experience of the Word of God through *lectio*. The average lay person does not have the leisure to spend a long period of time with the Office of Readings, save perhaps on Sundays and holidays. Such leisure may come with retirement, when the contemplative dimension of life can be more fully enjoyed not only for our own benefit but for that of the whole Body of Christ the Church. For those in the midst of our fully active years of life when many duties make their demands upon us, we may have to restrict our *lectio* or our Office of Readings to five or ten minutes. (At least let us give it equal prominence if not equal time with reading the newspaper and watching television; it does put what we receive through them in its true context.) We need not worry about this restriction of time. The Lord can give us all we need for the day, our daily bread, in an instant, if only we really want it and are open to receive it. The priority we give to *lectio* is more important than the duration.

But the priority will usually be reflected in some way in the duration.

As I have said, the aspect of watching should not be wholly absent, even when the Office of Vigils is changed into an Office of Reading. We always long for the coming of the Lord. The Church has continued to urge monks and nuns to observe this office as a vigil, a watching in the night. This has a particular power and poignancy about it, this watching in the night. Anyone who has watched through the night beside the bed of a sick one knows what I mean. We wait for the dawn, for a new day, and for the hope and promise it brings. The sun with its light and warmth is a natural sacrament of the Son with his illuminating revelation and his warming love. Watching in the night is a value we can come to know only by experience. Such watching gives a new dimension to all the other watching and waiting in our lives. Therefore it is something worth paying a price for. The expansion of consciousness that we can grow into by even a small amount of watching makes it truly worthwhile. Normally healthy adults can afford to miss an hour's sleep once a week or rise a couple of hours early on a Saturday or Sunday — promising themselves a nap later in the day if need be. When all is relatively quiet (I am aware some cities never seem truly quiet) there is an openness to the divine. When all others in our house sleep we have a special freedom to be to the Lord. A Thursday night watch with Jesus in Gethsemani — *Can you not watch one hour with me?* — can powerfully open space for God in our lives. Knowing the transforming value of watching I simply make suggestions here. In your creativity you can find ways of incorporating this value into your own life if you want to. Once you do, if you persevere with it long enough to discover something of what it has to give us, watching in the night will become an important part of your journey, however restricted your watching has to be and no matter how much that costs.

Watching, with hymns, psalms, and readings, is one of the ways we sanctify the hours.

LAUDS AND VESPERS

The cardinal hours of the day are those moments when darkness gives way to light and when light in its turn gives way to darkness. All religious traditions seem to sense that these are sacred times, times to be given to prayer. "In the morning I will praise you.... Let my evening prayer arise...."

The hope and promise of a new day calls forth praise. Christ has come again, in the sacrament of the rising sun: new light, new life, new hope. Christ will come again. Each new day is a pledge and promise of that. Life is full of possibility. The promise of Christ, of his revelation carries us beyond this. "For those who believe, all things are possible."

We do not know how to pray as we ought, so, as Saint Benedict wisely counselled, we begin with an earnest cry for assistance. After an initial cry for help Lauds often opens with a call to worship. "You who stand in the house of the Lord, lift up your hands to

the Lord. . . . " "Today, if you hear his voice, harden
not your hearts. . . . " This is followed by more reflexive
psalmody, psalmody that invites us to reflect upon the
wondrous goodness of our God, in himself and in what
he has done for his creation. Such reflection naturally
leads into psalms of praise and joyous thanksgiving. It
is customary in much of the Church to sing the canticle of Zechariah at Lauds. It heralds the dawning of
salvation; it bespeaks the hope of a "new day":

Blessed be the Lord God of Israel, for he has visited
and redeemed his people,
and has raised up a horn of salvation for us in the
house of his servant David,
as he spoke by the mouth of his holy prophets from
of old,
that we should be saved from our enemies, and
from the hand of all who hate us;
to perform the mercy promised to our fathers, and
to remember his holy covenant,
the oath which he swore to our father Abraham,
to grant us that we, being delivered from the hand
of our enemies, might serve him without fear,
in holiness and righteousness before him all the
days of our life.
And you, Child, will be called the prophet of the
Most High;
for you will go before the Lord to prepare his ways,
to give knowledge of salvation to his people in the
forgiveness of their sins,

through the tender mercy of our God, when the
    day shall dawn upon us from on high
to give light to those who sit in darkness and in
    the shadow of death,
to guide our feet into the way of peace.

Like every other office, Lauds has its reading and its
prayer, which often takes the form of a litany.

Vespers, the other cardinal hour, is not unlike Lauds,
though thanksgiving is more its theme: thanksgiving
for the graces of the day but also for all the graces of
salvation history. Mary's song of thanksgiving, an ex-
altation of true liberation, marks this hour and best
expresses its spirit:

My soul magnifies the Lord,
and my spirit rejoices in God my Savior,
for he has regarded the low estate of his hand-
    maiden.
For behold, henceforth all generations will call me
    blessed;
for he who is mighty has done great things for me,
    and holy is his name.
And his mercy is on those who fear him from
    generation to generation.
He has shown strength with his arm, he has
    scattered the proud in the imagination of their
    hearts,
he has put down the mighty from their thrones,
    and exalted those of low degree;
he has filled the hungry with good things, and the
    rich he has sent empty away.

He has helped his servant Israel, in remembrance
of his mercy.

THE DAY HOUR(S)

The current Liturgy of the Hours calls for only one "day
hour," seeking to adapt itself to the more demanding
work programs many today find ourselves subjected
to. It keeps a flexibility, though, based on the earlier
practice of three day hours: terce, sext, and none —
the third, sixth, and ninth hour (the hour that brought
Peter and John to the Temple). Pray-ers are welcome
to pause for this hour of prayer whenever it best fits
into their day. Hymns for the third, sixth, and ninth
hour are offered; the most appropriate can be chosen.
The hymns express the spirit of the particular hour and
invite the pray-ers to enter into it.

Terce, the third hour, around nine o'clock, is the
time when the Holy Spirit descended upon the apostles who were gathered fearfully in the upper room after
Jesus' ascension. This outpouring of the Spirit and the
apostolic boldness that followed upon it is seen to her-
ald the birth of the Church. The hour calls for a renewal
of this outpouring even now:

> Come, Holy Spirit, ever One
> With God the Father and the Son;
> It is the hour our souls possess
> With your full flood of holiness.

Let flesh and heart and lips and mind
Sound forth our witness to mankind
And love light up our mortal frame
Till others catch the living flame.

Almighty Father, hear our cry
Through Jesus Christ our Lord most high
And with the Spirit Paraclete
Whose reign the endless ages greet. Amen.

Sext, the sixth hour, noon, is the time of transition, from morning to afternoon, from coming to fullness to waning. It bespeaks the march of time and the sway of God over all. At the same time, the height of noonday heat calls to mind the heat of passion. A composite prayer comes forth:

O God of Truth, O Lord of Might
Who order time and change aright
Who send the early morning ray
And light the glow of perfect day.

Extinguish now each sinful fire
And banish ev'ry false desire
And while you keep the body whole,
Shed forth your peace upon the soul.

None, three o'clock, the ninth hour, finds evening approaching. Our thoughts are turned toward ending, toward death:

O God, creation's secret force,
Yourself unmoved, yet motion's source,

Who from the morn till evening's ray
Through every change you guide the day.

Grant us, when this short life is past,
The glorious evening that shall last
That, by a holy death attained,
Eternal glory may be gained.

Grant this, O Father, ever one,
With Jesus Christ your only Son
And Holy Spirit whom we adore,
Reigning and blest forevermore. Amen.

We can keep each of these hours, if we would — and as monks and nuns do — or let these themes inform our more informal prayer as we pray through the day. Traditionally these three hours have been called "the little hours." They are seen as but moments of prayer, a pause to come to presence, to worship in the midst of our day's labor. Monks often celebrate them at the place of their work. They are meant to foster and encourage our constant prayer. Three brief hours, said perhaps at morning and afternoon coffee breaks and at lunch, might be more effective than a longer midday prayer in achieving this purpose. In either form we can pray with the Church.

These hours are structured much as the others. After the introduction, there is a hymn, psalmody, a brief reading, and prayer.

COMPLINE

Compline is the latest hour in more than one respect. It is the hour that completes the day. And it was the last liturgical hour to develop. It seems to have come out of a monastic practice of saying some psalms together in the dormitory just before retiring. It has become one of the most popular of the hours. This is due in part because it most conveniently fits into most people's day. Evening prayers, prayer before going to bed, are common. A certain eloquent beauty has grown up around the celebration of Compline in monasteries that invites participation from the neighbors and invites visitors to take this prayer home with them as a family or personal practice. Compline has, more frequently than the other hours, found its way onto the radio. The office is often chanted in darkness, lending a wondrous mystic air to it. Then it is concluded with one of the most beautiful chants we have in honor of the Holy Virgin, the Salve Regina — Hail, Holy Queen:

Hail, holy Queen, Mother of Mercy, our life, our sweetness and our hope.
To you do we cry, poor banished children of Eve.
To you do we send up our sighs, mourning and weeping in this valley of tears.
Turn, then, most gracious Advocate, your eyes of mercy toward us.
And after this our exile show unto us the blessed Fruit of your womb, Jesus.
O clement, O loving, O sweet Virgin Mary.

THE COMPONENTS

The essential components of the Prayer of the Hours are hymns and psalms, readings and prayer. If we invest in a breviary, all of these are laid out for us. We can use them, conscious of praying with the Church. We can use them selectively, as they best fit into our lives and nourish our praying with the Church. An important thing always to keep in mind is that the Prayer of the Hours is *prayer*. This is the important thing: that we are truly praying, that we are turned to the Lord in love. All the components of the liturgical hours have this as their one final purpose: to help us be more fully and more wholeheartedly to God in prayer. The words, even though they be in themselves divinely inspired, have no value if they are not in service of true prayer. Praying with the Church does not lie primarily in saying certain words approved by the Church and being used commonly by Christians throughout the world, inspiring though this be. Praying with the Church means, first of all, being one with the Church in faith and love and in that love being with the members to Christ our Head and with him to the Father in Holy Spirit. We use the hymns that belong to the common heritage of the Church, guided by the Church in our choice. We use the formulas of prayer to make common our sentiments. We use the common readings to share common inspiration. But we use all these insofar as they help us to pray. When we pray individually or in a particular group we use a certain freedom, employing these hymns, readings, and prayer formulas insofar as they help us now truly to pray and to pray with the Church.

It is not important that we say all the words, or even pray all the words. We pray with the Church and use the words to the extent that they truly help us to pray with the Church. Prayer does not lie in getting the words said. It lies in reaching out to God in love. The particular formulas guide us, inspire us, invoke in us common sentiments, encourage and strengthen us in the realization that we are praying with all the Church. If a few of the words lead us into a deeper prayer, let us not distract ourselves from that prayer by trying to say all the words. The words have served their purpose. Let us pray.

THE PSALMS

The psalms are more problematical. These are indeed inspired songs. They not only belong to our heritage; they are a part of the Sacred Scriptures themselves. They were sung by the Chosen People for centuries before Christ came. We have every reason to believe that they were sung by Christ himself in the synagogue at Nazareth, in his home there, in the Temple at Jerusalem and at other times and places. They were a part of his prayer to his Father. This alone recommends them to us.

Yet, taken literally , they sometimes breathe forth sentiments that are far from the sentiments of the heart of Christ, the Prince of Peace. They are the songs of a warring people of the Iron Age who came to nation-hood by slaying the firstborn of Egypt and wiping out the people of Canaan. They belong to an old and past dispensation when "an eye for an eye and a tooth for a tooth" was the accepted norm rather than "love your enemy, do good to those who hate you." Nonetheless, Christians have consistently continued to pray these poems through the centuries and the Church makes them an integral part, even the preponderant part, of its daily prayer.

The early Fathers who struggled with them have given us many suggestions on how we might pray them as Christians. Many of the psalms can be prayed in their full literal sense. They express sentiments wholly consistent with the Good News of our Lord Jesus. But in the case of a good number, we have to leave the literal meaning behind and seek some spiritual meaning. Jerusalem, Sion, becomes the Church. The enemies are Satan and sin and the evil that lurks in our own hearts.

This transposition of meaning, however, does not solve the whole problem for us. Even if, through much study and prayer, we are able to pray the psalms in this transposed sense, whenever it is needed, we yet do speak out the hateful sentiments that the psalms express. And these consciously or unconsciously have an impact upon us. Maybe this is one of the reasons why, after living almost twenty centuries in the new dispensation of the Prince of Peace, we are still a people so prone to war and violence. If our daily prayer, at least at some levels of our being, nurtures in us sentiments of violence and vindication, the transformative power of the Gospel of love is being undermined.

There is another consideration that comes more strongly to the fore today now that the Prayer of the Hours has become the more common prayer of the People of God and is celebrated in the vernacular. Even if we ourselves, through study, meditation, and prayer, have arrived at being able to transpose the sense of what we are saying in our prayer, we cannot be sure, in fact we can hardly expect, that all who hear our prayer and are perhaps seeking to enter into it are able to make the same transpositions. Public prayer, prayer that is open to all the public, needs to take care that it can be easily understood by all the public. Certainly it needs to take care that it is not leaving itself wide open to misinterpretation. When people enter our church and hear us praying, "Blessed are they who take your little ones and dash their heads against a stone," they may well wonder. At least they are not apt to say as did the Romans as they looked upon the early Christian community in prayer: See how these Christians love one another. Unless, maybe, they were tempted to say it in derision.

In our use of the psalms, then, we might well be selective. Some very beautiful psalms are marked with a few verses that express sentiments foreign to the Gospel. These verses could be omitted. Some psalms, referred to as the cursing psalms, are so full of vindication that they might best be wholly left out of our prayer. There are psalms that have mixed sentiments. These might better be used for meditation than for common public prayer. There still remain many wonderful psalms that serve well to ring out our joy or express our deep repentance and our trust in the Shepherd of Israel. They offer imagery with which we can easily relate, that can call forth from us a deeply human response. With selectivity we can find enough psalmody to give body to our participation in the Prayer of the Church, though we may want to enhance it with our use of the beautiful canticles of the New Testament as well as enrich it with our repertoire of truly Christian hymns.

The psalms will probably ever remain an important part of the prayer of the Christian community. They can be prayed in many ways. We can make their words and sentiments our own. We can enter into Jesus and pray them in his name: Jesus in himself, the carpenter at Nazareth or the rabbi at Jerusalem, or Jesus as the head of the body that is the Church. We can pray them as Church, as a people. Many of the sentiments apply more aptly to us as Church with members in the prison camps of China or suffering disparagement (to say the least) in the occupied territories of Israel. We can unite with Mary or Joseph, with the apostles or saints of any age. The psalms are our common prayer and their sentiments weave through our history. We can also, if we are so moved, let them, like the Hail Marys of the rosary, be simply background music, as it were, while we rest more deeply in the Divine. This is more possible and more common among those who pray them regularly in a choir. The words of the psalms, their poetry and their cadences are there to help us to pray, to be in communion and union with our God of love.

The Liturgy of the Hours is a prayer and a school of prayer standing ready to serve us, to help us respond to the evangelical command to pray always, to bring us into an experience of prayer that belongs to us as Church. It has the empowering reality that it is in a special way the prayer of the Church. When we take it up it not only inspires us to pray with the Church; in fact, the Church prays in us. There is a grace in this that helps us feeble pray-ers. We are in an illustrious company of pray-ers that reaches beyond this world and this time. Those who stood in the Temple in Jerusalem in the centuries long past and now sing in the Temple in the heavenly places sing now with us. Christ, our God, is among them. And his holy mother. To them and us are joined the many saints who took up this prayer in the centuries that have rolled by since Christ ascended to the heavenly choir. This company is without number.

The poverty of our prayer is clothed in the splendor and magnificence of theirs. We pray as one. If it is penitence we need, we have the Misereres of Magdalene and Peter, of Augustine, and de Liguori. We have the dances of David and his shouts of triumph on the lips of celebrants of every age. We have the music of the greatest of masters. (I shall never forget the first time I heard Vespers celebrated in Saint John Lateran on the feast of the dedication of this cathedral of the pope. Today, thanks to excellent sound recordings, we can pray with these masters even in our own homes.) We have the haunting melodies of the simplest of psalm tones. And we have Zechariah's Benedictus and Mary's Magnificat, all coming to a culmination in Jesus' Eucharistic prayer — to which we now turn our attention.

CHAPTER SEVEN

ULTIMATELY IT IS LOVE

We tend to see things one after the other: this event, that event, another event — a whole train of events moving along. It is only with difficulty that we see how things fit together and, even more, see the underlying unity and meaning and the ultimate expression of their value. God, who sees things as they really are, sees everything at the same time, all together. They are all present to him in his eternal NOW. He sees them, as it were, all piled up in one place rather than strung out — the way we tend to see them. And at the summit of all, giving meaning to all, is creation's greatest act of love. For it is love that matters.

That act of love that stands at the summit of creation and gives meaning to everything else in creation is the act of love whereby the very Son of God, hav-

ing entered into the creation as one of us, offered to
his Father, our God, the greatest thing in the creation,
his very own life. As he himself said: "Greater love than
this no one has than to lay down one's life for another."
He laid down his life for all us others. And the life
he laid down was the life of God himself, God's own
human life.

He laid that life down for us his friends, even though
we are totally unworthy of such love, even though we
are such unworthy friends. As he said the night before
he died: It is not we who have chosen him, it is he
who has chosen us. "I no longer call you servants but
friends." We do not have the sense to chose him as
our friend. Or maybe it's the daring or the humility
that we lack. Whatever holds us back, be it our pride
or our stupidity or our selfishness, the fact remains:
even while we were still alienated from him by sin he
chose us as his friends and he laid down his life for us.

One of the most wonderful expressions of his friendship is the Mass. In the Mass he gives us not only his
very self but also this supreme act of love, the summit
of all creation. For the Mass is Calvary. In the Mass
Christ has given us a ritual act whereby we can, as it
were, reach into God's eternal NOW and make present
in our "now" that supreme act of love whereby Jesus
offers his life to the Father for us. The greatest and
ultimate act of love that was present on Calvary, the
act of love that embraced all humanity and brought
it to the Father and brought the Father's embrace of
love to all of us, is made actually present any time anyone of us who has received the gift of priesthood from

the Lord celebrates the ritual act we call the Mass. It is the very same supreme act of love as it ever exists in God's eternal NOW. It is the same act of love that Jesus made present in the upper room at that last supper he shared with his chosen ones. It is present here and now, given to us, his members, as our act of love to be offered now to his Father, to unite us all to him and win his embracing love for us all as his beloved children.

This is the Mass, the Eucharistic Liturgy.

A DIALOGUE

Have you ever noticed how the Mass is structured? It is celebrated in the form of a dialogue — a dialogue with God.

As we come into God's presence, we are greeted and welcomed by the priest, who stands in the place of the Lord as the mediator of our praying community. We immediately feel the need to tell God we are sorry. We have failed in so many ways to live up to all the potential of what he gave us the last time we gathered for this Eucharistic Liturgy. We enter into a penitential rite, confess our sinfulness, and ask God's pardon. And graciously, through the presider, God speaks to us a word of pardon. Free from our burden of guilt we are ready to enter into the celebration.

Some days we feel particularly festive, so at this point we join with the heavenly hosts and break out into a song of joy: *Glory to God in the highest.*

The preliminaries are now complete; we get down to business. In the prayer, articulated by our leader, to which we add our "Amen," we tell God what we have come for, what we need, something of our hopes and fears. He in his turn sits us down: I have something to say to you. He speaks to us through the readings.

We listen to what he has to say and we respond: a responsorial psalm, an alleluia. Some days we respond with a profession of our faith, reciting the creed. More often we respond by again expressing our needs, perhaps more in detail, in the prayers of the faithful. Our essential response comes in the offertory. What we can hardly express in words, we express in symbol. We bring to the Lord some bread and wine, food and drink, what sustains our lives. In this we say to him we want to give him our very lives, all that we have and all that we are.

In response, in a most wondrous gesture, God shows what he wants to do for us. He takes our gift, symbol of ourselves, and changes it into his very self. Then in Communion he gives us his very self. The exchange is complete. It is dialogue in its fullest existential expression.

It is time to thank the Lord: the post-communion prayer. He in turn, blesses us and sends us forth to bring the fullness we have received to others. Thanks be to God!

THE IMPORTANCE OF THE OFFERTORY

The whole of the initial dialogue of the Mass leads up to the symbolic act of the offertory. It is unfortunate that often the congregation is distracted from this act and the act itself is poorly presented. The collection, if there is one in connection with the celebration, needs to be taken up before our leader, the presider, begins his ritual act. For this collection is a way in which we the participants enter into the offertory. The collection is a gathering of each one's symbolic gift, the fruit of our life and labor, to be brought to the altar along with the symbolic bread and wine. If we sing at this time, the song needs to be carefully chosen. If it is not expressive of the offering of the bread and wine or what they represent, it can distract from this very important moment in the communal celebration. The bringing of the bread and wine from the midst of the community gathered, if it is given due focus and carried out with dignity, can be a powerful moment in the life of the community and of all the individuals in the community. It is the culmination of an interaction with God in the course of which he has led us toward a complete "yes" to his inviting love, to a complete gift of self, an openness to transformation. When we give our all we are wide open and ready to receive ourselves back fully Christed. To the extent that we enter into the offertory are we open to the transformation of the Eucharist.

We want to be careful about adding other gifts to the essential symbolic gift of bread and wine. The danger is that we might be content with offering God some of the fruit of our lives: our hard-earned money, our flowers and fruits and creative products, and fail to give our very selves. If this is the case, there is little possibility that the Eucharistic Liturgy will be for us a transforming event.

God accepts the gift we bring, all that it symbolizes and the gift itself, the bread and the wine. God takes that bread and wine and, letting it retain its own form and appearance, the one we have given to it, he transforms it into his very self. The bread and wine, the fruit of the earth and our human labor, become God the Son in his humanity, offering himself to his Father in his supreme act of love. This transubstantiation symbolizes what he wants to bring about within each one of us: a true transformation so that we will be actually one with the Son, in his humanity and in his divinity. He places at our disposal (what an awkward way of saying it, but it is there for us) his supreme act of love so that we can unite with it and offer it to the Father as our act of love: *Through him and with him and in him all honor and glory are yours almighty Father in union with the Holy Spirit now and forever.*

There is a dimension to this union of our love with Christ's in the Eucharistic Liturgy that never ceases to amaze me. The love we bring to the Eucharistic offering today becomes one with Christ's, one with his in the eternal NOW of God, and so one with his on Calvary. Just as the love he offered on Calvary is present in the NOW of God and is made present on the altar now, so our love offered now in union with his on the altar is present with his in the NOW of God and is therefore present with his on Calvary—and in every Mass that will ever be offered. The love we bring to the Eucharist today is present on Calvary when Jesus actually hung on the cross and brought about the salvation of the entire human race. It is there to console him in his dereliction. It is there with Mary's love and John's and the Magdalene's. It is also in the upper room when Jesus first placed this symbolic act and gave to his first priests the power to do likewise—not only to place this act but also to pass on this amazing power to other priests and give them the power to pass it on even to us. Our love is present at the Masses John the Beloved offered with Mary, at the Masses in the catacombs and in all the hiding holes of later years, in the prisons of China today, in the cloisters and in the basilicas. It is present in every papal Mass and in every Mass offered by the saints. The love we bring to the Eucharist today is one with Jesus' love before the face of the Father at the summit of all creation.

Is there anything we can do in our entire lives that is more important, more sublime than this? This, of course, cannot be divorced from the rest of our lives. For we can bring only that love that is truly present in our lives and lived in all that we do. The love we live in all the little tasks of everyday life is the love we bring to the Eucharist and offer with Christ's love. We have no other. It can be no other.

HOLY COMMUNION

Communion is then a sacrament of what already is. When God comes to us within species that are to be wholly consumed and lost within us, he expresses the completeness of the union that has already taken place through the transforming power of love. We need a certain centeredness to celebrate the Eucharist. All the complexity of the rite, all the components need to be seen as centered upon this transforming union. Each has its role to play: the conversion and repentance, the prayer and listening to the Word. Our response with its renewal of faith, the gift of ourselves are all prerequisites to the transforming union that Christ's love wants to bring about with us. This Eucharistic encounter brings to completion that which is begun within us in baptism. This is why in the Byzantine Church and among adults in the Roman Church, baptism is always immediately followed by Eucharist.

All the other practices we have looked at are tending toward this union, opening us for it, preparing us to enter into it. It is the consummating love of Jesus in the Eucharist, which is that of Calvary, that makes this union possible and brings it about. Saint Teresa of Avila has said that the grace of transforming union is never received apart from the Eucharist. It is clear to see why this is so.

There is something incomplete in the symbolic ritual and in its power to dispose us when we receive the Eucharist outside of the Eucharistic celebration. We are in danger that our lack of disposition will inhibit our openness to receiving the fullness of what the Lord wants to give. The Lord is almost a beggar in that he so reverences the freedom he has given us that he never forces himself upon us. He wants this transforming union far more than we do. He has paid the price for it, one beyond our comprehension. Yet he responds to our freely chosen dispositions and pushes no further. His grace is ever ready to aid us, but we have the responsibility for our dispositions. The way we participate in the dialogue of the Mass, the way we live our lives, fosters our dispositions or inhibits them. The more present and open we are to the realities of the unfolding ritual, the more fully disposed we will be to enter into the offertory and receive Communion.

At this point only contemplation seems to be appropriate. Only a total openness beyond all concepts and images seems to be adequate to the reality. Even the word "Communion" seems to be redundant. "Union" already says "with," why do we need the "com"? It is like Hebrew poetry: we say the thing twice in an effort to surpass the superlative. The union the Lord would have with us is beyond union. At the Last Supper Jesus prayed that we might be one with him even as he is one with the Father. We know that the unity that Jesus has with the Father within the Trinity is an absolute albeit mysterious unity that preserves the distinction of the persons. So is the unity Jesus the Son would have with us. Our likeness goes even into the Trinity, where our two in one or many in one is like unto their three in one. What he always has been, we begin to be in union with him. What more can be said?

THE PRAYERS OF THE ROSARY

THE SIGN OF THE CROSS

In the name of the Father and of the Son and of the Holy Spirit. Amen.

THE APOSTLES' CREED

I believe in God, the Father almighty, the creator of heaven and earth, and in Jesus Christ, his only begotten Son, our Lord, who was conceived by the Holy Spirit, born of the Virgin Mary, suffered under Pontius Pilate, was crucified, died, and was buried. He descended into hell. The third day he rose again from the dead. He ascended into heaven and sits at the right hand of the Father. I believe in the Holy Spirit, the holy

catholic Church, the communion of saints, the forgiveness of sins, the resurrection of the body and life
everlasting. Amen.

OUR FATHER—THE LORD'S PRAYER

Our Father, who art in heaven, hallowed be thy name.
Thy kingdom come. Thy will be done on earth as it is in
heaven. Give us this day our daily bread. And forgive us
our trespasses as we forgive those who trespass against
us. Lead us not into temptation but deliver us from
evil. Amen.

HAIL MARY—THE ANGELIC SALUTATION

Hail, Mary, full of grace. The Lord is with you. Blessed
are you among women and blessed is the fruit of your
womb, Jesus. Holy Mary, Mother of God, pray for us
sinners now and at the hour of our death. Amen.

GLORY BE TO THE FATHER—THE DOXOLOGY

Glory be to the Father and to the Son and to the Holy
Spirit as it was in the beginning, is now and ever shall
be, world without end. Amen.

THE FATIMA PRAYER

O Jesus, forgive us our sins, save us from the fires of hell. Lead all souls to heaven, especially those who are most in need of your mercy.

HAIL, HOLY QUEEN — THE SALVE REGINA

Hail, holy Queen, Mother of Mercy, our life, our sweetness and our hope. To you do we cry, poor banished children of Eve. To you do we send up our sighs, mourning and weeping in this valley of tears. Turn, then, most gracious Advocate, your eyes of mercy toward us. And after this our exile show unto us the blessed Fruit of your womb, Jesus. O clement, O loving, O sweet Virgin Mary.

Pray for us, O Holy Mother of God.

That we may be made worthy of the promises of Christ.

Let us Pray.

Pour forth, we beseech you, O Lord, your grace into our hearts, that we to whom the incarnation of Christ your Son was made know by the message of an angel, may by his passion and cross be brought to the glory of his resurrection, through the same Christ, our Lord. Amen.

ALTERNATE MYSTERIES OF THE ROSARY

THE HIDDEN LIFE

1. *Jesus' Submission to Mary and Joseph* (Luke 2:51–52). The wonder of God-become-human humbly obeying two of the fallible creatures that he himself has made.

2. *Jesus Works with Joseph as a Carpenter* (Mark 6:1–6). The humble, helpful apprentice, divine wisdom, learning from a man. God working with his hands, knowing blisters and splinters, an aching back and a sweaty brow.

3. *Jesus within the Extended Family* (Matt. 13:53–58). God living such an ordinary life in the village that no one noticed him.

4. *The Death of Joseph*. Scripture only implicitly tells us of this. Jesus knew what it was to be the only son of a widow.

5. *Jesus' Parting from Mary* (Matt. 12:46–50). A painful but challenging and loving separation — for our sakes.

JESUS' ENCOUNTERS WITH MARY DURING THE PUBLIC LIFE

1. *Cana* (John 2:1–12). He can't say no nor can he say the child's yes: no codependency here.

2. *Jesus' Visit to Nazareth* (Luke 4:15–30). Moments of maternal pride and moments of maternal terror and heartbreak for a loving Relative and Friend.

3. *"Behold My Mother and My Brothers...."* (Matt. 12:46–50). Perhaps only Mary understood it was not a rejection.

4. *"Blessed is the womb...."* (Luke 11:27–28). Again, the Most Faithful One understood.

5. *At the Cross* (John 19:25–27). We all have a mother in Mary who gave birth to us in agony.

VOCATION

1. *The Search* (John 1:35–39). Come and see.

2. *The Call* (Mark 1:17–20). Come, follow me.

3. *Fidelity* (Luke 9:57–62). He who looks back is not worthy.

4. *Betrayal* (Matt. 26:47–50). Betraying the Son of Man with a kiss.

5. *Fidelity to the End* (John 21:18–22). You follow me.

TABLE TALK

1. *At Levi's* (Matt. 9:9–13). He came for us sinners.

2. *At Simon's* (Luke 7:36–50). Love is what matters.

3. *At Bethany* (Luke 10:38–42). There are different vocations.

4. *Again at Bethany* (John 12:1–8). Jesus wants us to act extravagantly toward him.

5. *At the Cenacle* (John 13–17). Jesus pours out his heart and gives us the gift of himself in the Eucharist.

"I AM" — JESUS' SELF-IDENTITY

1. *"I Am the Bread of Life"* (John 6:35).

2. *"I Am the Gate"* (John 10:9).

3. *"I Am the Good Shepherd"* (John 10:14).

4. *"I Am the Way, the Truth and the Life"* (John 14:6).

5. *"I Am the True Vine"* (John 15:1).

THE HEALING MYSTERIES

1. *At Simon Peter's* (Matt. 8:14–17). Jesus has complete command over sickness.

2. *The Man Lowered through the Roof by His Friends* (Mark 2:1–12). Jesus listens to the prayers of friends.

3. *The Man with the Withered Hand* (Mark 3:1–6). Jesus can be angry and he is angry when we use others.

4. *The Ten Lepers* (Luke 17:11–19). Jesus is sensitive to gratitude.

5. *The Blind Man at Jericho* (Mark 10:46–52). Jesus is not put off by our importune cries.

JESUS' MINISTRY TO WOMEN

1. *The Woman Who Touched His Garment* (Matt. 9:20–22). A cruelly induced shame made her hide but she couldn't hide from Love. Her faith made her shine.

2. *Jairus's Daughter* (Mark 5:21–43). Such power, such dignity, such humanity in this Healer.

3. *The Widow of Naim* (Luke 7:11–17). Some needs speak for themselves. A mother needs her only son yet for love of us he deprived his own mother.

4. *The Adulterous Woman* (John 8:3–11). Where was the man? Jesus wouldn't stand for such injustice.

5. *"She has shown such great love "* (Luke 7:36–50). Love is what matters, and Jesus let women show their love in a woman's way.

THE EUCHARISTIC MYSTERIES

1. *The Manna in the Wilderness* (Exod. 16:4–36). Sweetness on a hard journey, but just enough for each day.

2. *Cana* (John 2:1–12). Water becomes wine as wine will become blood to celebrate our divine nuptials.

3. *The Multiplication of the Loaves* (John 6:1–15). In the hands of the apostles and their successors there is food for all.

4. *The Last Supper* (Mark 14:22–25). This is my body. This is my blood.

5. *The Meal at Emmaus* (Luke 24:28–32) They recognized him in the breaking of the bread.

THE FORETYPES OF THE RESURRECTION

1. *Elijah Raises the Widow's Only Son* (1 Kgs. 17:17–24).

2. *Elisha Raises the Son of the Shunammite* (2 Kgs. 4:8–37).

3. *Jonah Comes Forth from the Whale after Three Days and Nights* (Jonah 2:1–11).

4. *Jesus Raises the Son of the Widow of Naim* (Luke 7:11–17). Jesus himself, the only son of a widow.

5. *Jesus Raises Lazarus* (John 11:1–45).

JESUS' RESURRECTION

1. *On the Road to Emmaus* (Luke 24:13–35). "We had hoped" — the Scriptures as a source of hope.

2. *Easter Night* (Luke 24:36–43). "Have you anything to eat?" — the humanity of Jesus.

3. *A Week Later* (John 20:24–29). "Blessed are they who have not seen and have believed."

4. *By the Sea* (John 21:1–23). Peter humbled that he might be exalted.

5. *On Olivet* (Luke 24:50–53). Go tell all. He will return.

RECONCILIATION

1. *"A heart contrite and humble, O God, you will not spurn"* (Ps. 51:19).

2. *"Her many sins are forgiven because of her great love"* (Luke 7:47).

3. *"Neither do I condemn you"* (John 8:11).

4. *"Father, forgive them. They do not know what they are doing"* (Luke 23:34).

5. *"If you forgive anyone's sins they are forgiven"* (John 20:23).

APPENDIX C

A SIMPLE OFFICE

MORNING PRAYER

O Lord, open my lips....
And my tongue shall proclaim your praise.
Glory be to the Father and to the Son and to the
   Holy Spirit
as it was in the beginning, is now and ever shall
   be. Amen.

HYMN

PSALMS

*Choose three psalms from the Book of Psalms in your
Bible.*
At the end of each Psalm:

Glory be to the Father and to the Son and to the
Holy Spirit as it was in the beginning, is now and
ever shall be. Amen.

151

READING

Read a passage from your Bible — perhaps from the Old Testament or the first reading of today's Mass — and reflect on it.

CANTICLE OF ZECHARIAH (Luke 1:68–79)

Blessed be the Lord, the God of Israel,
for he has visited his people, he has set them free.
And he has established for us a saving power,
in the house of his servant David,
just as he proclaimed,
by the mouth of his holy prophets from ancient
    time,
that he would save us from our enemies
and from the hands of all those who hate us,
and show faithful love to our ancestors,
and so keep in mind his holy covenant.
This was the oath he swore to our father Abraham,
that he would grant us, free from fear,
to be delivered from the hands of our enemies,
to serve him in holiness and rightness
in his presence, all our days.
And you, little Child,
you shall be called Prophet of the Most High,
for you will go before the Lord to prepare a way for
    him,
to give his people knowledge of salvation
through the forgiveness of their sins,
because of the faithful love of our God

in which the rising Sun has come from on high to
visit us,
to give light to those who live in darkness and in
the shadow of death
and to guide our feet into the way of peace.
Glory be to the Father and to the Son and to the
Holy Spirit
as it was in the beginning, is now and ever shall
be. Amen.

PRAYER

Let us humbly and confidently bring our concerns
to God.

For the Church..., let us pray to the Lord.
Lord hear our prayer.
For those serving in authority..., let us pray to the
Lord.
For our loved ones..., let us pray to the Lord.
For our special needs..., let us pray to the Lord.
For our departed..., let us pray to the Lord.

Let us pray as our Lord has taught us.

Our Father, who art in heaven, hallowed be thy
name. Thy kingdom come. Thy will be done on
earth as it is in heaven. Give us this day our daily
bread. And forgive us our trespasses as we forgive
those who trespass against us. Lead us not into
temptation but deliver us from evil. For thine is
the kingdom and the power and the glory, now and
forever.

God of infinite compassion and mercy, hear the prayer of your people. Bless this day, fill it with your peace and love. Make us sacraments of your love in the world. Grant this through Christ, our Lord.

Amen.

Let us bless the Lord.
And give him thanks.

MIDDAY PRAYER

O God, come to my assistance.
O Lord, make haste to help me.
Glory be to the Father and to the Son and to the
    Holy Spirit
as it was in the beginning, is now and ever shall
    be. Amen.

HYMN

PSALMS

Choose three psalms from the Book of Psalms in your Bible.

READING

Read a passage from your Bible — perhaps from the Epistles of Saint Paul or the first reading at Mass — and reflect on it.

PRAYER

Let us pray as our Lord has taught us.

Our Father, who art in heaven, hallowed be thy name. Thy kingdom come. Thy will be done on earth as it is in heaven. Give us this day our daily bread. And forgive us our trespasses as we forgive those who trespass against us. Lead us not into temptation but deliver us from evil. For thine is the kingdom and the power and the glory, now and forever.

Lord, in the fullness of the day, we come to you. Bless our labors, make them fruitful for your glory and for the well-being of all the human family. Grant this through Christ, our Lord.

Amen.

Let us bless the Lord.
And give him thanks.

EVENING PRAYER

O God, come to my assistance.
O Lord, make haste to help me.
Glory be to the Father and to the Son and to the
    Holy Spirit
as it was in the beginning, is now and ever shall
    be. Amen.

HYMN

PSALMS

Choose three psalms from the Book of Psalms in your Bible.

READING

Read a passage from your Bible — perhaps from the Gospels or the Gospel of today's Mass — and reflect on it.

CANTICLE OF MARY (Luke 1:46–55)

My soul proclaims the greatness of the Lord
and my spirit rejoices in God my Savior;
because he has looked upon the humiliation of his
    servant.
Yes, from now onward all generations will call me
    blessed,
for the Almighty has done great things for me.
Holy is his name,
and his faithful love extends from age unto age to
    those who fear him.
He has used the power of his arm,
he has routed the arrogant of heart.
He has pulled princes from their thrones and
    raised high the lowly.
He has filled the starving with good things,
sent the rich away empty.

He has come to the help of Israel his servant, mindful of his faithful love.
— according to the promises he made to our ancestors —
of his mercy to Abraham and to his descendants for ever.
Glory be to the Father and to the Son and to the Holy Spirit
as it was in the beginning, is now and ever shall be. Amen.

PRAYER

Let us humbly and confidently bring our concerns to God.

For the Church . . . , let us pray to the Lord.
  Lord hear our prayer.
For those serving in authority . . . , let us pray to the Lord.
For our loved ones . . . , let us pray to the Lord.
For our special needs . . . , let us pray to the Lord.
For our departed . . . , let us pray to the Lord.

Let us pray as our Lord has taught us.

Our Father, who art in heaven, hallowed be thy name. Thy kingdom come. Thy will be done on earth as it is in heaven. Give us this day our daily bread. And forgive us our trespasses as we forgive those who trespass against us. Lead us not into temptation but deliver us from evil. For thine is the kingdom and the power and the glory, now and forever.

God of love, we thank you for the gift of this day with its many blessings. Forgive us for all the ways in which we have failed to use them well. Give us a peaceful night and the rest we need. Grant this through Christ, our Lord.

Amen.

Let us bless the Lord.
And give him thanks.

SELECT BIBLIOGRAPHY

Listening — Scriptural Prayer

Amiot, F. *From Scripture to Prayer: Daily Readings from the Gospels and St. Paul.* Staten Island, N.Y.: Alba House, 1957.

Avery, Benedict R. *Daily Bible Reading with the Church.* Collegeville Minn.: Liturgical Press, 1952.

Grollenberg, Lucas H. *Believing Makes Sense: A Way of Reading the Bible.* London: SCM Press, 1983.

Havener, Ivan. *Spiritual Reading of Scripture.* Collegeville, Minn.: Liturgical Press, 1979.

Keating, Thomas. *Awakenings.* New York: Crossroad, 1990.

Love, Julian P. *How to Read the Bible.* New York: Macmillan, 1940.

Lupton, Daniel E. *A Guide to Reading the Bible.* Chicago: ACTA Publications, 1959.

McKenzie, John L., ed. *New Testament for Spiritual Reading.* New York: Herder & Herder, 1969.

Martin, George. *Reading Scripture as the Word of God: Practical Approaches and Attitudes.* Ann Arbor, Mich.: Word of Life, 1975.

Muto, Susan A. *Approaching the Sacred: An Introduction to Spiritual Reading.* Denville, N.J.: Dimension Books, 1973.

———. *A Practical Guide to Spiritual Reading.* Denville, N.J.: Dimension Books, 1976.

——. *The Journey Homeward: On the Road of Spiritual Reading*. Denville, N.J.: Dimension Books, 1977.

Pennington, M. Basil. *Monastery*. San Francisco: Harper & Row, 1983.

Poelman, Roger. *How to Read the Bible*. New York: Guild Press, 1966.

Van Kaam, Adrian L. *The Woman at the Well*. Denville, N.J.: Dimension Books, 1976.

Decades of Roses — The Rosary

Bryan, David Burton. *A Western Way of Meditation: The Rosary Revisited*. Chicago: Loyola University Press, 1991.

Burnside, Eleanor T. *Bible Rosary: The Life of Jesus, Thirty-Five Mysteries*. Birmingham, Mich.: Rosary Thirty-Five, 1981.

De Montfort, St. Louis. *The Secret of the Rosary*. Trans. Mary Baerbour. Bay Shore, N.Y.: Montfort Fathers, 1954.

Haffert, John M. *Sex and the Mysteries*. Washington, N.J.: Ave Maria Institute, 1970.

London, Larry. *The Seven-Day Scriptural Rosary*. Huntington, Ind.: Our Sunday Visitor, 1988.

Marcucci, Domenico. *Through the Rosary with Fra Angelico*. Staten Island, N.Y.: Alba House, 1987.

Paul VI. *Devotion to the Blessed Virgin Mary: Marialis Cultus*. Washington, D.C.: United States Catholic Conference, 1974.

Pennington, M. Basil. *Praying by Hand*. San Francisco: Harper-Collins, 1991.

Ward, J. Neville. *Five for Sorrow, Ten for Joy: A Consideration of the Rosary*. Garden City, N.Y.: Doubleday, 1973.

Wilkins, Eithne. *The Rose-Garden Game: A Tradition of Beads and Flowers*. New York: Herder & Herder, 1969.

William, Franz Michael. *The Rosary: Its History and Meaning*. Trans. Edwin Kaiser. New York: Benziger, 1953.

Walking in His Way — The Stations of the Cross

Bories, Marcel. *Life through the Cross, Meditation on the Way of the Cross Based on the Seven Sacraments*. New York: Desclee, 1954.

Berrigan, Daniel. *Stations: The Way of the Cross*. San Francisco: Harper & Row, 1989.

Charpentier, Etienne, and Marc Joulin. *Five Roads to the Cross according to the Gospels*. Trans. Margaret Lydamore. London: SCM Press, 1983.

Houselander, Caryll. *The Way of the Cross*. New York: Sheed & Ward, 1955.

John Paul II. *The Way of the Cross*. New York: Catholic Near East Welfare Association, 1982.

McCarroll, Tolbert. *A Way of Cross*. New York: Paulist Press, 1985.

Marmion, Columba. *The Way of the Cross: Its Efficacy and Practice*. St. Louis: B. Herder, 1960.

Nisbet, Jim. *An Illustrated Stations of the Cross: The Devotion and Its History*. Mystic, Conn.: Twenty-Third Publications, 1982.

Nouwen, Henri J. M. *Walk with Jesus: Stations of the Cross*. Maryknoll, N.Y.: Orbis, 1990.

Raymond, M. *New Way of the Cross*. Milwaukee: Bruce, 1952.

Sheen, Fulton J. *The Way of the Cross*. Garden City, N.Y.: Garden City Books, 1932.

Storme, Albert. *The Way of the Cross: A Historical Sketch*. Jerusalem: Fransciscan Printing, 1976.

Underhill, Evelyn. *The Path of Eternal Wisdom: A Mystical Commentary on the Way of the Cross*. London: Watkins, 1948.

Van Zeller, Hubert. *The Way of the Cross*. Springfield, Ill.: Templegate, 1958.

Another Tradition — The Jesus Prayer

Brianchaninov, Ignatius. *The Prayer of Jesus*. London: J. M. Watkins, 1965.

Chariton of Valamo. *The Art of Prayer*. London: Faber & Faber, 1966.

Gillet, Lev. *The Jesus Prayer*. Crestwood, N.Y.: St. Vladimir's, 1987.

Hausherr, Irenee. *The Name of Jesus*. Trans. Charles Cummings. Kalamazoo, Mich.: Cistercian Publications, 1978.

Maloney, George A. *The Prayer of the Heart*. Notre Dame, Ind.: Ave Maria Press, 1981.

———. *Centering on the Lord Jesus: The Whole Person at Prayer*. Wilmington, Del.: Michael Glazier, 1982.

———. *The Jesus Payer for Modern Pilgrims*. Seal Beach, Calif.: Contemplative Ministries Publications, 1988.

Sofrony, Archimandrite. *His Life Is Mine*. Crestwood, N.Y.: St. Vladimir's, 1977.

Vogel, Arthur A. *The Jesus Prayer for Today*. New York: Paulist, 1982.

Ware, Kallistos. *The Power of the Name: The Jesus Prayer in Orthodox Spirituality*. Oxford: SLG Press, 1977.

The Way of the Pilgrim and the Pilgrim Continues on His Way. Trans. Helen Bacovcin. Garden City, N.Y.: Image Books, 1978.

Winkler, Gabriele. *The Jesus Prayer in Eastern Spirituality*. Minneapolis, Minn.: Light and Life, 1986.

Transformative Being — Centering Prayer

The Cloud of Unknowing and the Book of Privy Counselling. Ed. William Johnston. New York: Doubleday, 1973.

Deonise hid Divinite and Other Treatises on Contemplative Prayer Related to the Cloud of Unknowing. Ed. Phyllis Hodgson. London: Oxford University Press, 1955.

Johnston, William. *The Mysticism of the Cloud of Unknowing*. St. Meinrad, Ind.: Abbey Press, 1975.

Keating, Thomas. *Open Mind Open Heart*. Warwick, N.Y.: Amity House, 1986.

Keating, Thomas, et al. *Finding Grace at the Center.* Still River, Mass.: St. Bede's, 1978.

Maloney, George. *Inward Stillness.* Denville, N.J.: Dimension Books, 1976.

Main, Lawrence. *Moment of Christ: The Path of Meditation.* London: Darton, Longman & Todd, 1984.

Merton, Thomas. *Contemplative Prayer.* New York: Doubleday, 1971.

Nemeck, Francis K., and Marie T. Coombs. *Contemplation.* Wilmington, Del.: Michael Glazier, 1982.

Pennington, M. Basil. *Daily We Touch Him.* New York: Doubleday, 1977.

———. *Centering Prayer.* New York: Doubleday, 1980.

———. *Centered Living.* New York: Doubleday, 1986.

———. *Call to the Center.* New York: Doubleday, 1990.

———. *The Way Back Home.* New York: Paulist, 1990.

Moments That Mark the Hours —
The Prayer of the Hours

Bradshaw, Paul F. *Daily Prayer in the Early Church: A Study of the Origin and Development of the Divine Office.* New York: Oxford University Press, 1982.

Dalmais, Irenee H., et al. *The Liturgy and Time.* Collegeville, Minn.: Liturgical Press, 1986.

Dugmore, C. W. *The Influence of the Synagogue on the Divine Office.* Westminster: Faith Press, 1964.

General Instruction of the Liturgy of the Hours. Washington, D.C.: U.S. Catholic Conference, 1983.

Pennington, M. Basil. *Prayertimes: Morning — Midday — Evening: A Pocket "Liturgy of the Hours" for All Christians.* New York: Doubleday, 1987.

Taft, Robert F. *The Liturgy of the Hours in East and West.* Collegeville, Minn.: Liturgical Press, 1986.

Ultimately It Is Love — The Eucharistic Liturgy

Balasuriya, Tissa. *The Eucharist and Human Liberation*. Mary-knoll, N.Y.: Orbis, 1979.

Bermejo, Luis M. *Body Broken and Blood Shed: The Eucharist of the Risen Christ*. Chicago: Loyola University Press, 1986.

Bernadot, Marie V. *The Eucharist and the Trinity*. Wilmington, Del.: Michael Glazier, 1977.

Bernier, Paul. *Bread Broken and Shared: Broadening Our Vision of Eucharist*. Notre Dame, Ind.: Ave Maria, 1981.

Burghardt, Walter J. *Seven Hungers of the Human Family*. Washington, D.C.: USCC, 1976.

Cabie, Robert. *The Eucharist*. Collegeville, Minn.: Liturgical Press, 1986.

Deiss, Lucien. *It's the Lord's Supper: The Eucharist of Christians*. New York: Paulist, 1975.

Farrell, Edward J. *Celtic Meditations: Moments of Thanksgiving, Invitation to Eucharist*. Denville, N.J.: Dimension Books, 1976.

Feeley-Harnik, Gillian. *The Lord's Table: Eucharist and Passover in Early Christianity*. Philadelphia: University of Pennsylvania Press, 1981.

Gelineau, Joseph. *The Eucharist Prayer: Praise of the Whole Assembly*. Washington, D.C.: Pastoral Press, 1985.

Guthrie, Harvey H. *Theology as Thanksgiving: From Israel's Psalms to the Church's Eucharist*. New York: Seabury, 1981.

Haring, Bernard. *The Eucharist and Our Everyday Life*. New York: Seabury, 1979.

Hellwig, Monica. *The Eucharist and the Hunger of the World*. New York: Paulist, 1976.

John Paul II. *The Mystery and Worship of the Holy Eucharist*. Vatican City: Polyglot Press, 1980.

Jasper, R. C. D., and G. J. Cuming, eds. *Prayers of the Eucharist: Early and Reformed*. New York: Pueblo, 1987.

Kilpatrick, George D. *The Eucharist in Bible and Liturgy*. New York: Cambridge University Press, 1984.

Heron, Alasdair I. *Table and Tradition: Toward an Ecumenical Understanding of the Eucharist*. Edinburgh: Handsell, 1983.

O'Connor, James T. *The Hidden Manna: A Theology of the Eucharist*. San Francisco: Ignatius Press, 1988.

Pennington, M. Basil. *The Eucharist Yesterday and Today*. New York: Crossroad, 1984.

————. *Breaking Bread: The Table Talk of Jesus*. San Francisco: Harper & Row, 1986.

Sheerin, Daniel J. *The Eucharist*. Wilmington, Del.: Michael Glazier, 1986.